SELF-HELP WORKBOOK

EVERYTHING AT YOUR OWN PACE

The Definitive Guide To Help You Overcome Your Fears, Anxieties, and Deepest Worries By Learning How To Love Yourself Whole-Heartedly

Elian Carter

Copyright © 2020 Elian Carter

All Rights Reserved

Copyright 2020 By Elian Carter - All rights reserved.

The following book is produced below with the goal of providing information that is as accurate and reliable as possible. Regardless, purchasing this eBook can be seen as consent to the fact that both the publisher and the author of this book are in no way experts on the topics discussed within and that any recommendations or suggestions that are made herein are for entertainment purposes only. Professionals should be consulted as needed prior to undertaking any of the action endorsed herein.

This declaration is deemed fair and valid by both the American Bar Association and the Committee of Publishers Association and is legally binding throughout the United States.

Furthermore, the transmission, duplication or reproduction of any of the following work including specific information will be considered an illegal act irrespective of if it is done electronically or in print. This extends to creating a secondary or tertiary copy of the work or a recorded copy and is only allowed with express written consent from the Publisher. All additional right reserved.

The information in the following pages is broadly considered to be a truthful and accurate account of facts and as such any inattention, use or misuse of the information in question by the reader will render any resulting actions solely under their purview. There are no scenarios in which the publisher or the original author of this work can be in any fashion deemed liable for any hardship or damages that may befall them after undertaking information described herein.

Additionally, the information in the following pages is intended only for informational purposes and should thus be thought of as universal. As befitting its nature, it is presented without assurance regarding its prolonged validity or interim quality. Trademarks that are mentioned are done without written consent and can in no way be considered an endorsement from the trademark holder.

Table of Contents

PART I 11

Chapter 1: What is Holding You Back 12

   Why People Procrastinate 12

      Abstract Goals 14

      Not Having Foreseeable Rewards 15

      A Disconnect from Our Future Selves 15

      Being Too Optimistic 16

      Being Indecisive 17

      Task Aversion 17

      Perfectionism 18

      Self-Handicapping 18

   Other Major Reasons for Not Getting Things Done 19

      Not Sure What to do 20

      There is No Deadline or Accountability 20

      Don't See Any Consequences 21

   Why Getting Things Done is Critical 21

Chapter 2: It's Time to Get Things Done 24

   Overcoming Procrastination 24

      Don't Catastrophize 24

      Focus on Your "Why" 25

      Get Out Your Scheduler 25

      Be Realistic 26

      Break it Down 26

      Stop With the Excuses 27

- Find an Accountability Partner 27
- Optimize Your Environment 27
- Forgive Yourself 28
- Mindfulness Meditation Technique 28
  - Body Scan Meditation 29
  - Sitting Meditation 29
  - Walking Meditation 29
  - Simple Mindfulness 30
- 15 Habits of Highly Productive People 30

Chapter 3: Visualizing a Better Future 33

- How to Visualize Your Future 33
- More Tips for Visualization 34
  - Visualize Your New Life 34
  - Create a Vision Board 35
  - Write Down Your goals 35
  - Let Yourself Zone Out 35
  - Say Your Goals Out Loud 36
  - Think About What You Want and not What You Don't Want 36
- Life When You Get Things Done 36
  - A Feeling of Relaxed Control 37
  - Your Thinking Will Be Stimulated 37
  - More Organization and Less Clutter 37
  - Less Time for Worry 38

PART II 40

Chapter 1: Self-Confidence In Various Situations 41

- How a Lack of Self-Confidence Affects Us 42

Chapter 2: Social Anxiety 44

Social Anxiety and Lack of Confidence In Specific Situations 45

Chapter 3: Learning to Become Comfortable 50

  Building Your Self-Confidence 50

    Groom Yourself Regularly 51

    Photoshop Your Self-Image 51

    Destroy Negative Thoughts 51

    Get to Know Yourself 52

    Be Kind and Generous 52

    Be Prepared 52

    Know Your Principles and Live By Them 53

    Speak Slowly 53

    Stand Up Straight 54

    Increase Your Competence Levels 54

    Set Small Goals and Achieve Them 54

    Change Small Habits About Yourself 54

    Focus Your Attention on Solutions 55

    Become Active 55

    Gain More Knowledge 55

  Overcoming Procrastination 56

  Build Confidence At Work 58

Chapter 4: Getting Rid of Social Anxiety 61

  Chapter 1: Knowing Anger 66

    Understanding Anger 68

  Chapter 2: The Physiology and Psychology of Anger 71

    The Physiological Impact of Anger 71

    The Psychology of Anger 72

  Chapter 3: Why Anger Management Is So Important 74

Impact of Anger on Mentality 74
Impact of Anger on Emotions 75
Impact of Anger on Spirituality 75
Dangers of Ignoring Anger Management 76

Chapter 4: Correct Assessment of Your Anger Issues 78

Chapter 5: Understanding Simple Ways to Manage Anger 82

Chapter 6: Mindfulness and Anger Management 97

The Way to Seek Happiness, Inculcate Compassion, Gain Control of Emotions, and Channelize Anger Positively 97

Mindfulness Is the Practice of Being Aware 98

Four Important Principles in Mindfulness 99

Chapter 7: 8-Week Anger Alleviation Plan 102

Ditching the Autopilot 102

Learning to Sense and Feel to Become Aware 103

Meditation and Exercise 104

Learning to Recognize Negative Thoughts and Mindful Walking 104

Allowing Things to Be- Without Reacting Impulsively 105

Every Thought Is Just a Thought 106

Learn to Be Kind to Yourself and Others 107

Becoming Mindful in Your Routine 107

Chapter 1: Back to the Basics 110

Chapter 2: Unlocking Your True Purpose Through Mindfulness 114

Re-centering Yourself 114

Giving Your Emotions Space 116

Making Clear Decisions 117

Keeping Yourself Safe 117

Improving Relationships 118

Fostering True Joy 120

Chapter 3: Moving Mindfully in Daily Life 122

    Coming to the Present Moment: Daily Guided Mindfulness Meditation With Journaling (Week 1) 122

    Coming to the Present Moment: Daily Guided Mindfulness Meditation With Journaling (Week 2) 126

    Coming to the Present Moment: Daily Guided Mindfulness Meditation With Journaling (Week 3) 128

    Mini Meditation Toolbox: 15 Quick and Easy Meditations to Integrate Mindfulness Into Your Daily Life 131

    Mini Meditation Toolbox: 10 Quick and Easy Meditations to Ease Stress, Depression, Addiction, Anxiety, Pain, Distraction, and Loss Using Mindfulness 140

Chapter 1: Understanding Panic Attacks and Panic Disorders 148

    What Is a Panic Attack? 149

Chapter 2: Anxiety and Panic Attacks Aren't the Same 154

Chapter 3: Biological and Psychological Causes of Panic Attacks 158

    Biological Causes of Panic Attacks 158

    Psychological Causes of Panic Attacks 161

Chapter 4: Who Is At a Greater Risk of Panic Attacks? 163

Chapter 5: Tips to Cope With Panic Attacks When They Strike 165

    Ways to Prevent Panic Attacks 165

Chapter 6: The 8-week Plan to Deal With Panic Attacks 170

    Identify the Triggers, Fears, and Problematic Behavior 170

    Identify Your Negative Thought Patterns 172

    Dissociate From the Negative Thought Patterns 174

    Facing the Fears Head-on 175

    Practice Relaxation 176

    Practice Mindfulness 178

    Getting the Experience 179

PART I

Chapter 1: What is Holding You Back

The first half of this book focused on the negative aspects of clutter and how removing unnecessary items from your life can be cathartic in so many ways. The goal of all of this was to begin getting things done in your life. This includes all aspects of a person's personal and professional life. Honestly, decluttering was just the first step. It was a way to clear up our minds and reduce distractions. After doing this, it is time to start moving forward and getting things done in our lives. Now that our physical and mental spaces are clear, what else can we focus on? The goal of this chapter is to present some of the biggest challenges to getting things done.

Why People Procrastinate

Procrastination is something many people in our society suffer with. It is the purposeful and unnecessary delay of actions or decisions. Why do something now when you can just do it tomorrow? Well, because you never know what tomorrow will bring. Other challenges will arise, distractions will come up, and you will continue to load up your plate because you refuse to take things off of it. Since you are making the excuse today for waiting until tomorrow, what is stopping you from making the same excuse tomorrow, or the next day and the next day?

Imagine being at a buffet and loading up your plate. When you go to sit down, you decide not to eat much of the food because you want it later. Instead, you go and grab another plate to fill up and bring back to the table. Now, you have two plates to finish, and you have no idea how you will do it. Eventually, the restaurant is about to close, and you don't have the time or space to finish everything. You will most likely waste a large portion of the food. This is what procrastination looks like in life. You keep pushing things back until you become overloaded, overwhelmed, and very close to the deadline, if you even make it at all.

Procrastination is one of the worst enemies of getting things done. It really has no value, except for the fact that some people thrive on making quick deadlines. However, you will also be more likely to make big mistakes. You will never be able to complete the work to your full potential because so many things will be missed. Even if they're minor, they still add up.

Procrastination leads to so many missed opportunities too. Several people do not pursue their goals because they put them off for too long. Eventually, they get to the point where they lose interest or become too involved in other things to where they no longer have time.

People assume that procrastination has everything to do with will power. While this can be a major reason, for sure, it is not the only one that exists. There are many deeper reasons for why people put things off. There are some psychological aspects that are at play. For example, anxiety and fear of failure will terrify people into paralysis. Nobody wants to fail, and if they start something, failure is a huge possibility. As a result, we delay starting anything. At least then, we can save face a little bit.

When our motivation to complete a task outweighs the negative aspects, then there's a strong chance we will still finish it. However, if the negative aspects outweigh our own motivation, then we will put off pursuing a goal if we even do so at all. The following are some other factors that keep up from moving forward. If we follow these, we will always procrastinate.

Abstract Goals

If a person has a vague or abstract goal, then they are more likely to procrastinate. They are not excited enough about it. In fact, they might not even know what the goal is, as there is no clear definition. For example, making a promise to get fit is an abstract goal. It is a simple statement with no real substance. What are the chances you will get fit if you have no actual plan in place for doing so? Furthermore, what does "get fit" even mean to? Does it mean losing a certain amount of weight, gaining muscle, looking slimmer, having more energy, or a combination of all? Honestly, you are not even giving yourself a chance to obtain this goal, as you will just put it off until you forget about it.

A more solid goal would be, "I will lose 15 pounds within two months and be able to run six miles by then." This is a concrete goal with real values and end results. From here, you can create specific action steps to get there. For example, losing two pounds and increasing your run mileage by one every week. Once you create real goals with a legitimate plan, then you are more likely to not put things off.

Not Having Foreseeable Rewards

Many individuals put things off because they see no actual rewards in the near future. For example, a teenager may not attend college because he or she cannot fathom waiting four years or more to get a degree in something that might make them money. In addition, the money will not come right away, which is another deterrent.

People often want immediate pleasure rather than long-term success. This can be seen in people neglecting to create savings or investment accounts. They do not want money later; they want it now. As a result, they delay setting up one of these essential accounts because they can't see the benefits they will create in the future.

This same mindset can apply to punishments, as well. The farther into the future a punishment is, the less likely it will motivate someone to take action. If you are studying for a final exam in college and it is months away, you are not that concerned about it, because even if you fail, it will be a while until that actually happens.

A Disconnect from Our Future Selves

People tend to procrastinate because they cannot comprehend a connection between their present and future selves. They believe the two individuals are mutually exclusive for some reason and don't realize that they are creating their future person by the actions you take today.

A person may delay starting a healthy diet because they cannot see themselves overweight and dealing with chronic diseases in the future. A company someone works for has a chance of going out of business, but the employee does not work on his resume because he cannot see himself being out of work. In both of these examples, their present and future selves are completely different people.

Being Too Optimistic

Now, being optimistic is not a bad thing; however, getting to the point where you overthink your abilities can be a problem. This is a common occurrence as many people do not work on tasks in the present because they highly believe they can complete it in the future. While this may be true, there will still be an increased amount of stress and anxiety. Also, the potential for oversight and significant errors will be present.

Imagine that you have a 10,000-word paper due to Friday, and it is only Monday. It would make sense to write 1,000-2,000 words daily, instead of waiting until Wednesday or Thursday. When writing the paper ahead of time, you will have extra opportunities to think everything through, and also go back and edit your work. Giving yourself extra time will help you in creating quality work.

Being Indecisive

This is when you cannot make a move because you cannot decide what course of action to take. For example, you may hesitate to apply for a job because you cannot decide which one is best for you. This is a phenomenon known as analysis paralysis, and it has stopped many great people right in their tracks. The following are some factors that make it difficult to make a decision.

- The more options you have, the harder it will be to decide a preferable path to take.
- The more similar different options are, the harder it will be to choose. You might end up analyzing the smallest sectors of each choice.
- The more important the decision is, the harder it will be to make because of the impact it will have on you and others.

It is best if you can keep your decisions to a minimum, as well as your choices. Each time you make a decision, you deplete your mental resources to a degree. So, if you make a host of decisions in a short time period, you have a high likelihood of getting burned out.

Task Aversion

People often procrastinate because they are not looking forward to a task they need to perform. For example, they might have to call them back to resolve a payment dispute but are not looking forward to talking with a customer service representative. As a result, They put off doing it. If you are avoiding a task because of the aversion you have to it, you are just delaying your agony. Imagine how good you will feel after doing it. So, hold your nose and get it done.

Perfectionism

People often want things so perfect that they are terrified of doing something out of fear of the mistakes they will make. Instead of starting and taking their chances, they avoid moving forward. Perfectionism has been called the enemy of productivity because of all the delays it creates along the way. People do not realize that things will no be perfect, so they waste excessive time trying to ake things this way.

Self-Handicapping

Many individuals are terrified of exposing their lack of ability for something. As a result, they procrastinate so they can use it as an excuse for poor performance. They would rather that people think they're lazy than incapable. Procrastinators with this mindset are more likely to put things off if they feel that failure will reflect badly on them.

These are some of the most common reasons for procrastination. There is no easy answer to why people avoid doing things, but it must be overcome for people to start accomplishing things. The following are a few more reasons for procrastination:

- Self-sabotage
- Low self-efficacy
- Perceived lack of self-control
- Fear of being criticized

Sometimes, there are more urgent situations, like ADHD, depression, or low self-esteem, that need to be addressed. The better question to ask is: Why put something off until tomorrow if I can get it done today?

Other Major Reasons for Not Getting Things Done

For some reason, people are just not getting as many things done as they could. Now, I am not saying you have to be on the go all the time. That is not healthy, either. What I am saying is that you need to accomplish things within a certain time period, or you will never achieve anything in life. This will not just affect you, but those who rely on you, as well, like employees, business partners, and family members. To make the world go around, people need to get things done. Yet, they don't. I already spoke about procrastination as a major factor. I will now detail a few other reasons why this happens.

Not Sure What to do

Many people do not do anything because they have no idea what they should do. Even if they have a goal, they are clueless about how to get started in any way. This often occurs because we see other people's accomplishments but have no idea how they achieved them. We keep trying to guess but can't figure it out. Even if we do become aware of how something was accomplished, the values do not line up with our own, which makes us even more confused. It is better to keep on track with your own beliefs when trying to accomplish a goal, rather than rejecting them completely. Rejecting your values will make you even more confused.

There is No Deadline or Accountability

Accountability seems to be going by the wayside these days. People don't get things done because they are not expected to. There is often no disciplinary actions taken, so people continue to lack the drive to move forwards.

Also, when deadlines are nonexistent, then there is no need to get moving. Either we don't create deadlines for ourselves, or other people don't place them on us. If you work for someone and they do not set deadlines, then the operations of the company are not very sound. If you do not set your own deadlines for goals, then you need to start doing so. Make them concrete and not too far out. Remember, you don't want to fall into a procrastination step.

Set a specific date for when you want to accomplish something and stick to it completely. Set it around important events if you can. For example, if you are planning a vacation or will be attending a concert, make it a goal to finish a certain project or reach a specific endpoint. If you are attending a wedding, and you also need to get in shape to fit into your suit, you can make a goal to lose 10 pounds prior to the wedding.

Don't See Any Consequences

This goes along the lines of accountability, but the reason so many people don't get things done is that they do not realize the consequences until they already occur. For example, if your roof needs to be fixed, you will probably put it off because you do not see any consequences for doing so. Of course, on the night that it's pouring rain and the roof suddenly collapses, you will recognize your mistake. Start seeing the potential consequences of not getting things done. Write them down if you have to. Once you see them visually, then you are more likely to take them seriously. For example, if you need new tires on your car and you have been putting it off, then write down that you will get stranded on the freeway with four ruptured tires.

Why Getting Things Done is Critical

Here is the bottom line. The many advancements we have made in this world were done by go-getters who acted constantly. They were not done by people who refused to do the work. As you look back on history, any type of accomplishment, whether good or bad, had massive action behind it. I say bad, as well, because there have been many negative events in our history. I hope you keep your goals positive.

Getting things done creates a sense of accomplishment. No matter how much or how little you do today, it is far better than doing nothing. Nothing gets you nowhere while small steps create some progress.

Getting things done now is the ultimate productivity hack available. There are no tricks or secret formulas. It is simply a matter of doing something now, rather than nothing at all. Whatever you can manage to do within a given period of time, do it, and you will be that much closer.

Imagine having to paint a house. This is not an easy task, especially if you have a big house. Let's say, for this example, the house has 100 walls to paint. If you pain one a day, that is still something. After 100 days, which is just over three months, you will have painted the whole house. Taking three months is better than nothing at all. On certain days, when you have more time and energy, you can paint extra on those days. If painting your house is a goal, then give yourself a deadline with rewards or punishments along the way. For example, if you are not halfway done by a certain date, then cancel something you were looking forward to. Hold yourself accountable, and if you need to, have someone else hold you accountable too.

In the next chapter, I will cover many different tips to start getting things done.

Chapter 2: It's Time to Get Things Done

Now that I have covered the reason why people don't get things done; it is now time to start taking action. This chapter will be focused on various strategies to overcome the blocks in your life. Start following these, and you will be accomplishing things in no time.

Overcoming Procrastination

It's time to stop putting things off. Many of your dreams and goals have gone unfulfilled because you waited too long to start working on them. The world has also missed out on your gifts because you had the potential to create something great if you only took some action in completing it. The following are some ways to overcome one of the greatest obstacles to not getting something done: Procrastination.

Don't Catastrophize

This means that you make a bigger deal out of things than you should. This could be based on the results you might get, or the excruciating the actual task will be. In any event, you are expecting the process to be unbearable.

Here's a little tip: it won't be. We often overthink to the point that our mind creates a scenario that is not conducive to reality. The truth is, hard work, boredom, and other challenges will not kill you. You may not enjoy them on time, but you will overcome them. Also, the results we get are rarely ever at the level we imagine them to be. The thought of a fall is generally harder than the fall itself.

Always believe in yourself that you can make it through something and deal with the consequences, positive or negative, that come with it. The truth is, you can. Even if a task is as horrible as you imagined, you got through it, and it's out of the way. This is much better than thinking about it. Just get it done!

Focus on Your "Why"

You "why" is the ultimate reason for you doing something and should be used as a motivating factor for you. Many procrastinators focus on short-term gains and do not pay attention to long-term potential. This is why it's important to remember your "why." It is the end result you are expecting.

This can be used for any goal in your life, personal or professional. If you have been putting off creating a resume, then imagine yourself in your dream job. If you have been putting off organizing your room, imagine how good you will feel when you can find things easily and don't have to get around a huge mess.

Get Out Your Scheduler

Projects often do not get done because people make no time for them. They will do it when they have time, and therefore, the time will never come. You need to make time and stick to it. Get out your scheduler, whether it's an online planner, paper planner, or calendar, and start blocking off times. Whatever important tasks that need to be completed, write them down and on a specific time and date. Unless something unavoidable comes up, stick to the specific block on your schedule. When people write things down, they are holding themselves accountable. If they miss doing something, they can look at it, and it will remind them.

Be Realistic

Getting things done means you are setting yourself up for success. Do not create unrealistic goals for yourself. Set an achievable goal, and then take specific action steps to get there. For example, do not tell yourself that you will start working out five times a week in the morning immediately when you are not even a morning person. Instead, set up your workout schedule in the evening. If you ultimately want to work out in the mornings, then you can start by doing it once a week and then increasing your days. Do not expect to reach your goals instantly. Set up a long-term plan for success.

Break it Down

Tasks can often become overwhelming, and this leads to procrastination. Break them down into smaller and more manageable tasks with specific deadlines for each small task. If you are planning to landscape your home, start with a small area and give yourself the time you need in each section.

Stop With the Excuses

Here it goes: You will never be fully energized; it will never be the right time; you will often not be in the mood; conditions may never be perfect. Stop using these as excuses. Waiting for any of these will just delay you for no reason. Getting things done is not about waiting for the perfect opportunity. It is about using what you ave to create opportunity. Stop with the excuses!

Find an Accountability Partner

It can be difficult to hold yourself accountable, so find a partner to help you. Express what your goals are to this person and the deadlines that you have. Your accountability partner can then follow up with you and make sure you are staying on track. If you don't reach your deadlines, your partner's job is to grill you as to why. You guys can help each other in this manner to make it a mutual relationship.

Optimize Your Environment

Your environment will play a huge role in creating distractions. Optimize it by finding a quiet place and only having the things you absolutely need. Turn off the TV, social media (I recommend logging out so you can't access it easily), get rid of any papers or clutter that will catch your attention. How many times have you meant to start something, only to get distracted by something else? This is very common, and you must do what you can to avoid it happening to you.

Forgive Yourself

While it might be true that starting something earlier would have been more advantageous, do not beat yourself up for not doing so. You cannot change the past, so forget about it. You can make up for it though by taking advantage of the present. Learn from your past mistake of putting something off and start doing things today. If you should have gone to college five years ago, well, it's okay. You can still go now.

Procrastinators are often trying to avoid distress, but in doing so, they are ironically creating more of it. Start taking the action steps I have described above, and you will no longer be putting things off until tomorrow.

Mindfulness Meditation Technique

Many individuals are not able to get things done because they cannot live in the present moment. They are either anxious about the past or worried about the future. Both of these are unproductive thoughts to have and must be eliminated immediately. You must start focusing on the present, and mindfulness meditation techniques are a great way to do so. Bear in mind, it can take years to master the practice of meditation, so I will just go over the basics to get you started. The following are some structured meditation exercises.

Body Scan Meditation

Start by lying down on your back with your arms at your sides, palms facing up, and legs extended. Now pay close attention and observe every section of your body from head to toe. Become fully aware of any sensations or emotions you are feeling and from where they are coming from. This will bring awareness to yourself and what is happening to you. You will begin living in the present moment with real-time feelings.

Sitting Meditation

Sit in a comfortable position, preferable in a chair, with your back straight, feet flat on the floor, and your palms on your lap. Once in a comfortable position, breathe in slowly through your nose and allow it to go down to your diaphragm. Then slowly let the breath out. Focus completely on your breathing. If you get distracted by anything, note the experience and then return your attention back to your breathing.

Walking Meditation

Find a quiet space that is at least 15-20 feet in length. Walk slowly between each wall in the room and focus completely on the experience. Be aware of all of the subtle movements that are being used to keep you balanced. Do not pay attention to anything else but your walking.

Simple Mindfulness

The following are a few more mindfulness exercises. These are simple and can be practiced anywhere.

- Focus on your breathing. Take slow and deep breaths in and out. This was done in the meditative position but can also be accomplished standing up anywhere.
- Find joy in the simple pleasures of life and live in the moment.
- Accept yourself and learn to treat yourself like you would a good friend.
- Experience the environment you are in with all of your senses. Do not be in such a rush all the time. Fully taste the food you're eating, stop to smell the roses, listen to the birds chirping, and even touch some dirt. Feel your surroundings.

15 Habits of Highly Productive People

To become successful, you must mimic the habits of other successful people. The following are effective habits that productive people use every day. These individuals get things done, and you can, as well.

- Focus on the most important tasks first. These are the ones that have the most urgency, the closest deadlines, and the most with the most severe results if not done. Complete them first and then move on to other things.
- Cultivate deep work, which are your hardest, most boring, and most complicated tasks. They have to be done, and if you are not focused fully, they will be missed. Say "no" to people more often, limit distractions, set up a scheduled time for these tasks each day, and go where you do your best work, whether in the office, library, or café, etc.
- Keep a distraction list. While you are working, anytime a distraction comes up, write it down, and then get back to work. This technique works because you are giving attention to your distraction, which eases up its strength over you.
- Use the 80/20 rule. Determine the 20% of your work that requires the most attention. Look at the remaining 80% and see what you can cut out to make more time for the 20%.
- Take scheduled breaks. Even though you want to get a lot done, you cannot just work 24/7. Take scheduled breaks throughout your workday and spend the rest of the time being fully focused. For instance, spend 55 minutes working hard, then take a 10 minutes break to relax and eat something.
- Limit the number of decisions you have to make. Decisions that aren't important should not take up too much of your time or energy. For example, many productive people will wear similar outfits every day because their wardrobe is not as important as other decisions.

- Eliminate insufficient communication. Ignore and delete useless emails, do not engage in too much idle chatter, and avoid gossip, which is a complete waste of time.
- Delegate certain tasks when you can. If you are busy with your career, then you can hire people to do things like take care of your lawn or do your dry cleaning.
- Learn from your successes, as well as your mistakes. Even in success, lessons can be learned about making things more efficient.
- Plan as much as you can for things going wrong because getting caught off guard can be quite a time consumer. It is better to have a plan ahead of time than trying to come up with one urgently.
- Don't wait until you are inspired or motivated to work. Start working and get yourself inspired or motivated.
- Avoid Multitasking. Instead, focus on one task for as long as you can before moving over to the next one.
- Get enough sleep, eat well, exercise, and take time to recharge. This will give you the energy you need when it's time to be productive. Whenever you do something, put all of your effort into it, including rest.
- Take time to get better at tasks by educating yourself and improving your skills.
- Manage your time and energy. Do not waste any of them unnecessarily.

Once you start taking these action steps seriously, you will notice yourself accomplishing a lot more. I will now get into looking towards your future and the life you want to create.

Chapter 3: Visualizing a Better Future

When you learn to get things done and do them well, you will create a better future for yourself. This can become one of your motivations to get moving, as well. In this chapter, I will continue to focus on action steps to get you moving so you can get things done. Once you can visualize your future, you can create it.

How to Visualize Your Future

In this section, I will go over some ways to visualize your future so that you can create an image that inspires you. This is a powerful tool that helps you create the future you want. Will it turn out exactly as you see it? Definitely not. There are too many variables that factor in. However, always keeping that picture in mind means that you will push yourself harder to achieve the success you want. As you see your reality a few years down the line, you will expect more out of yourself. Start by answering the following questions. Remember, these are the answers you hope to give five, 10, 15, or whatever years down the line.

- When someone asks you what you do for work, what do you tell them?
- Describe all of your surroundings in great detail, including your house, the city, neighborhood, and what's nearby. Where do you spend most of your free time?
- What is the atmosphere like at work and in your home, and how do you contribute to it?
- What is your greatest accomplishment? What brings you the most pride?

- Are there any regrets that you have?
- What are the specific steps you took to get where you are?
- What advice would you give to someone else who wants to be where you are?
- What problems arose along the way?

After answering these questions, you will understand where you want to be and have an idea of how to get there.

More Tips for Visualization

Once you begin visualizing your future, then you have it ingrained in your mind. It becomes much harder to let it go. Of course, this does not mean that it's a guarantee. You still must put in the work and make the right moves. For example, if you want to start a business, you can picture the type, how big it will be, where it should be located, how it will look, and whether you plan to have employees or not, among other things. Seeing is believing, though, and the following tips will help you start believing in yourself and your future.

Visualize Your New Life

One way to become excited about your goals is to imagine what your life will be like when you achieve them. For example, if you plan on increasing your salary, imagine that extra money coming in. How much will it be, and what will you be able to do with it? What will you be doing to get that extra money, whether it's through work, investing, or starting a business, etc.? Anything you can imagine about what your life will be like, try to picture it in your mind.

Create a Vision Board

Start collecting images, quotes, articles, and any other visual representations that you feel reflect your future. For instance, you can collect a specific item from a state if you plan on living there someday. This will help you trigger inspiration and hold you accountable for your dreams.

Write Down Your goals

This is a common practice and is touted as being very effective by most productive people. If you are not fond of vision boards, you can write down your goals in lieu of that practice. You may also do it in conjunction with each other for added benefits.

Let Yourself Zone Out

If you find yourself daydreaming at certain times, let it happen. Your mind is trying to tell you something about what you want. Many geniuses in the past, including Einstein, would zone out throughout the day. During these moments, a bolt of inspiration can strike, and great plans can be made. Of course, you cannot daydream all the time, or nothing will get done, which defeats the purpose.

However, when you can, take the time to do it.

Say Your Goals Out Loud

Whatever you have planned, whether short-term or long-term, say it out loud, so the universe knows. This also triggers your brain to understand what you want, so it also starts thinking towards that direction.

Think About What You Want and not What You Don't Want

There is a phenomenon known as the Law of Attraction. According to the rules, what you focus on is what the universe delivers to you, even if you're thinking about it in a negative way. So, even if you're thinking about poverty in terms of not falling into it, you will still attract it because it is in your mind. Therefore, it is better not to even visualize poverty but just think about becoming wealthy.

Life When You Get Things Done

All the information and strategies I have gone over in this book lead up to one thing: Getting things done. That is how you achieve what you want in life. You simply must take action and go for what you want. The action steps in the previous chapters provide a way to make goal-getting easier by providing direction, focus, and motivation. I will end this book by over the many benefits of getting things. Getting things done, or GTD is an actual process and state of mind. When you start incorporating it, you will notice many changes during and after.

A Feeling of Relaxed Control

You will feel in control of your life because you are taking active steps to create it. This may be the number one benefit of getting things done. Performing frequent assessments, processing information, and acting on it can make your mind feel like it's water, where it just flows and makes decisions naturally. It takes time for everyone to get to this state.

Your Thinking Will Be Stimulated

When you get things done, your thinking will be stimulated in advance. You will continuously be thinking about the little and big projects in your life, and they will rarely if ever, slip by you. Procrastination will be an afterthought, and you will always be ahead of the curve.

More Organization and Less Clutter

Getting things done means you will clean off your desk literally and figuratively. You will accomplish your tasks and keep your work area organized too. When you get things done, you will be more versatile, and it will become easier to make and keep commitments. In addition, you will be able to keep others accountable for their commitments.

Less Time for Worry

Thinking is good, but overthinking can be detrimental. It can lead to worry, anxiety, and fear. One of the best ways to avoid this is by acting. Worrying occurs when you have a moment for it. When you act, you are doing and have less time to worry.

The entire point of getting things done is just that, getting things done. This is how you accomplish your goals and start living the life you imagine. There are so many get-rich-quick schemes and people promising others the world if they just do a few simple things. With this book, I wanted to provide many different action steps for you so you can tidy up, clear out unnecessary garbage, both emotional and physical, and start working on your dreams. It may take time, but if you're moving in the right direction, that is what matters most.

PART II

Chapter 1: Self-Confidence In Various Situations

"Each time we face our fear, we gain strength, courage, and confidence in the doing."

-Theodore Roosevelt

While we have been speaking of self-worth and self-value, the focus of this chapter will be self-confidence, which is a different subject altogether.

Self-confidence is when you have faith in yourself and your abilities in a particular situation, and it does not relate to overall self-worth. If your self-confidence levels are low, it is because you are not comfortable in a particular setting, for whatever reason.

To help make self-confidence more clear, here are a few scenarios that showcase it in different circumstances.

- A doctor is self-confident when he performs any type of procedure within his specialty. He has so much training and experience that he truly believes in his skills and abilities to perform in various situations at work. When this same doctor goes for a hike, he does not have the same level of confidence in conquering a high peak, because he is out of shape.

- A mechanic can fix any car with his eyes closed. He has been a mechanic for so many years, that he is confident there is nothing that will come into his garage that he cannot handle. When this mechanic tries to work on the plumbing in his home, he is not very successful and has no confidence in his ability to perform the tasks.

- A great artist is confident in his ability to paint a portrait. If you ask him to solve a math problem, he has no confidence whatsoever.

These examples showcase how self-confidence can truly be based on the state of affairs, depending on what a person is facing at the moment. To handle a situation well, you must have self-confidence in your ability to do so. Self-confidence is gained through training, education, repetition, and life experience. It is impossible to be confident in every situation you ever come across, but the more you are willing to learn, the more confidence you will gain throughout life.

How a Lack of Self-Confidence Affects Us

As I mentioned before, self-confidence is circumstantial and will impact various areas of your life differently. Depending on how much experience, knowledge, or training, we have in different aspects of life, our confidence will ebb and flow. The key is to have self-confidence in the important areas of our lives, where it really matters. There are many examples in our everyday lives where self-confidence will play a major role.

Regarding the work setting, people who lack confidence in this arena cannot perform their necessary duties at an adequate level. This means poor job performance, being overlooked for raises and promotions, and even being let go from a position. If a person performs their job well, low self-confidence can still impact their desire to move up the latter. If they are confident in their particular position but do not feel confident at a higher level, like management, then they won't go after the promotion. They will simply stay put, even though they have the potential to do more.

Concerning starting a business, a certain level of confidence is needed to perform numerous tasks. There are many independent skills involved in running a business, and chances are, you will be doing most of them yourself when you first start. You need to have the proper training and education in these different areas, like finance, setting a budget, and marketing, etc., or you will not succeed in them. If you feel you can't do them yourself, then you may have to higher someone to do so. It may be worth it to avoid errors.

Self-confidence matters in our personal lives too. In order to find friends or develop relationships, we must have confidence in our abilities to form them. For example, it takes a lot of confidence for a man to walk up to a woman and say, "hi." To make friends, you must have the courage to talk to people. To learn new things and experience a new adventure, you must also have confidence in yourself to perform them. Once again, confidence comes from experience, and the more you put yourself out there, the more confident you will become.

Confidence is crucial in specific social settings. For example, during a work meeting, a lack of confidence can hold you back from speaking up, even if you have something very important to say. You won't get the necessary information out there that many people in the meeting could receive value from. This also relates to socializing with friends. You may have a friend who is harming themselves, but because you are uncertain how they will react, you ca nothing. You do not have the confidence that you will be able to respond appropriately.

A lack of confidence does not allow you to communicate assertively, which is important in order to get what you want. Instead of asking for things directly, you will beat around the bush and hope that the person will pick up on your clues. You will also use minimizing language, like "Sort of" or "kind of." This type of communication makes it seem like you lack conviction, and no one will take you seriously. You will just appear weak. Being assertive is essential, whether you are asking for something at working or setting boundaries with your friends.

If you suffer from low self-confidence, then every aspect of your life will suffer. We will get into different ways of increasing your confidence in the next chapter. For now, we will discuss how self-confidence works in different settings, especially in those that create anxiety for everybody.

Chapter 2: Social Anxiety

For this chapter, I will provide more detail for a specific type of confidence issue, and that is social anxiety.

Social Anxiety and Lack of Confidence In Specific Situations

Social anxiety is an actual disorder where a person has a phobia in which a person feels like they are being watched and judged by everybody. There may be select situations where this is actually happening, but in most circumstances, it is an unfound fear. This is an extreme situation where a person has a lack of confidence in everything they do, and therefore, feel like they are the center of attention.

Going for a job interview, taking a test, going on a date, or speaking in public are normal things that create anxiety in almost everybody. It is amplified greatly in someone who has a social anxiety disorder. Furthermore, these individuals actually become nervous during normal, everyday activities like shopping for food, parking their car, or using a public restroom. Their anxiety is so intense that they feel judged in every moment of their lives. This fear can become so strong that it interferes with people going to work, attending school, talking to their friends, or doing any other menial task during the day.

It is estimated that about seven percent of the American population suffers from social anxiety. While this number is not massive, it shows that the problem is not uncommon.

Researchers believe there is a genetic component where areas of the brain that deal with fear and anxiety are involved. However, there is no explanation as to why some family members are affected while others are not. For example, out of two siblings, one may be shy and quiet, while the other one is loud and bombastic.

Another cause of social anxiety may be underdeveloped social skills. Some individuals will feel discouraged after talking to people, even if the conversation did not go poorly, which will cause them to avoid interactions in the future. The lack of interaction will just lead to further underdeveloped social skills, and the social anxiety trend will continue.

Many people with this disorder do not have anxiety in specific social settings, but instead in areas where performance is involved. This is often referred to as performance anxiety and is related to performing in front of a crowd in any type of capacity, whether it is a speech, dance recital, or sporting event. Speaking in public is one of the worst fears that people have, and in some surveys, it is number one. Jerry Seinfeld used to make the joke that during a funeral, most people would rather be inside the casket than the ones giving the eulogy.

Even if a person is confident in the subject matter, having to discuss it in a large crowd, with hundreds, or even thousands, of eyes, looking at them, will create a high level of anxiety. This situation would be unsettling for many people. There are many reasons why someone would have a fear of speaking in public, and it goes beyond just being nervous.

Fear and anxiety will create a physiological response within us. During this process, our autonomic nervous system, which works as a protective mechanism by keeping us alert, will make us hyper-arousable. Generally, this is done to put the body in a state of battle. As a result, we will have an emotional experience to fear, which will interfere with our ability to perform well in front of an audience.

Another factor to consider is the person's beliefs about the speaking engagement. Many people will feel that if they screw up something in front of a crowd, it will hurt their credibility, and therefore, their careers. They also feel that their performance will never be forgotten, and their whole public image will be destroyed in an instant. The fact that everyone has a camera on their phones lends some more credibility to this fear. These feelings cause people to overthink and become extremely anxious beyond their control.

Anxiety during a public speech is greater in those who don't do it often. The more a person speaks in front of a crowd, the less nervous they become over time. Unfortunately, most people do not speak in front of audiences constantly, unless they do it for a living. If someone only speaks a few times a year or less, then they will usually have anxiety every time. Also, a person's status in relation to the audience members can play a role in their confidence levels. For example, if a person is speaking in front of high-level executives about a topic they already know, then this can create an immense amount of fear. They worry about having their speech dissected. What a person must realize here is that it is not so much the content of the speech, but how it is presented.

The most obvious reason for the fear of public speaking is the actual skill involved. Speaking in front of an audience involves getting the people engaged. This is done by proper timing, eye contact, stage presences, charisma, and a little bit of humor. The bottom line is, you must be able to connect with the audience somehow, or they will not care whatsoever what you have to say, no matter who you are. Your status may capture their attention for a while, but if you can't keep their attention, your speech will be forgotten before it even starts. Many people know this and are worried that they won't be able to hold their audience's attention.

The more anxious you are, the less likely you are to perform well. It is to your advantage to be as relaxed as possible and overcome your social anxiety, which is much easier said than done.

Aside from public speaking, another social situation that can cause anxiety is being in a large crowd. Many people with social anxiety are okay when they are just around their friends. However, once the circle starts increasing, their anxiety grows tremendously. This type of fear is known as enochlophobia, and it is related to the perceived dangers posed by large gatherings of people you may see in everyday life. The fear includes getting lost, stuck, or harmed in some manner by the crowd.

Most of you are probably thinking of concerts or other places where organized gatherings occur. The simple solution here would be to avoid these types of events. However, this fear also encompasses busy metropolitan areas, public transits like the bus or subway, or even workspaces with a lot of employees. Any type of space where a large number of people are, a person with this type of phobia will become fearful and anxious.

In the next chapter, we will describe various ways to build up your self-confidence, so you can be prepared to handle any situation, even if you are not familiar with it.

Chapter 3: Learning to Become Comfortable

When you lack self-confidence, it means you are unsure of yourself in a particular setting. You have a certain level of discomfort, which precludes you from going all-in when performing a certain task. Unfortunately, if your confidence levels are not high enough, then you will not perform at your highest level. This does not mean you aren't nervous or slightly anxious. It literally means that you do not believe in yourself in a specific situation.

A person will never feel fully confident in every aspect of life. There will be plenty of times when we are faced with something new, and it will completely throw us off our game. The goal of this chapter will be to build self-esteem in some of the most important areas of our lives and also develop the critical thinking skills we need to overcome almost any situation, no matter how unfamiliar it may be.

Building Your Self-Confidence

Nobody is born with an unlimited amount of self-confidence. Also, people are not born with zero confidence. It is something that either gets built-up or deteriorated over time. Unfortunately, many people have had their confidence shattered so many times that they never have confidence in themselves in any situation, no matter how familiar they are with it. The practices in this section will focus on building self-confidence in the general sense, so you are ready to attack life, no matter what gets thrown your way.

Groom Yourself Regularly

This may sound obvious, but many people do not realize how good they will feel when they take the time to shower, do their hair, clean their nails, and dress nicely. The old saying, "When you look good, you feel good," Holds a lot of truth. Even if you have nothing important planned for the day, take the time to groom yourself. You will automatically feel more confident in any situation you come across. You don't have to go to the salon every day or wear thousand-dollar suits. The goal is to look good when you observe yourself in the mirror. This could mean wearing your favorite shirt and jeans combination.

Photoshop Your Self-Image

We take a lot of stock in our self-image. No matter how much we try to say that looks don't matter, we like to look at ourselves in the mirror and see a positive self-image. You can alter your self-image by mentally photoshopping yourself in a way that is positive to you. You can then work on obtaining this image in real-life. For example, if you see yourself 20 pounds lighter, then keep this image in your mind and work towards it.

Destroy Negative Thoughts

No matter how unfamiliar you are with a situation, you are more likely to handle it well if you get rid of your negative thoughts. These simply take up space in your mind and have no value in your productivity. Be aware of our self-talk and how you think about yourself. This may sound ridiculous, but when you find a negative thought entering your mind, picture it as an object or creature that you want to destroy. For example, when you begin having negative thoughts, picture them as bugs. Now, squash those bugs mentally, and you will effectively destroy your negative thoughts. This is a great mental trick to play on yourself. After getting rid of the negative thought, replace it with a positive one.

Get to Know Yourself

When going into battle, it is best to know your enemy very well, no matter who they are. When you are dealing with low self-confidence, your enemy becomes yourself. This is why it is important to get to know yourself as well as you can. Listen intently to your thoughts, write about yourself in a journal, determine what thoughts about yourself dominate your mind, and analyze why you have negative thoughts.

Next, write down all of the positive aspects that you have, no matter how minuscule they may seem. Start thinking about the limitations you have and determine if they are real and verified, or just something you came up with in your head. Dig as deep you can get into your psyche, and you will find out more about yourself than you had ever known. The more you know about yourself, the greater self-confidence you will have.

Be Kind and Generous

Be kind and generous to others, whether it is time, money, or other resources, will be great for improving your self-image. When you are genuinely able to help someone when they need you, then it makes you feel good about who you are. It gives you a sense of purpose.

Be Prepared

Be as prepared for life as you can. Think about this for a moment: if you are taking an exam, and have not studied, then you won't be prepared, and your confidence level will be very low. On the other hand, if you did study intensely, then you will be much more prepared and have a greater amount of confidence. Imagine life as one big exam. The more prepared you are every day, the more confident you will feel in any situation. The following are some general ways you can be more prepared.

- Have plenty of food in the refrigerator and cabinets.
- Have a substantial emergency fund.
- Have the basics as far as emergency supplies at all times.
- If you have something specific planned for that day, like a presentation or meeting, be as prepared as possible for it.
- Always be on alert for dangerous situations.

Know Your Principles and Live By Them

What are the main principles upon which your life is built? If you are not sure, then it's time to sit down and really think about it. Otherwise, your life will be completely directionless. When you know your principles and live by them, then you are truly living your passion, and this is great for your self-confidence. People who are simply coasting through life with no real values will have no goals in life either. They are simply existing and not fully living. When you refuse to live your life based on your values, then you lack confidence in yourself.

Speak Slowly

Speaking slowly will make a huge difference in how people perceive you. It shows a sense of knowledge and confidence in what is being said. Someone who speaks with a rapid-fire approach generally does so because they are not confident in what they are saying. They just want to get the word out there and hope nobody calls them out. Even if you don't feel totally confident on a subject, try speaking slowly anyway, and see how much your self-confidence actually builds. This can be a great mind trick. When you speak slow, you have more time to formulate good thoughts. Of course, I am not telling you to take it to the extreme here, just don't spit words out like a machine gun.

Stand Up Straight

This is another simple trick to help you feel better about yourself. When you slouch, not only does it showcase a lack of confidence, you actually have less self-confidence. This goes along the lines of looking good and feeling good. And trust me, when you stand up straighter, you will look much better.

Increase Your Competence Levels

Simply put, if you are more competent in something, you feel more confident. You gain competence through practice and training. In any situation in life, get as much training as you can to feel as fully self-confident as you can. Let's use the example of a house fire. I hope that your house never burns down, but if it does, I want you to feel confident that you and your family can escape safely. Map out an escape plan and practice it as often as you can. Many companies do quarterly evacuation drills. Employ this same practice in your house. If an emergency like this ever occurs, you will have more competence, and therefore, confidence in being able to handle it. Think of as many possible circumstances as you can in life, and determine ways to practice and train in them.

Set Small Goals and Achieve Them

When you are able to achieve a goal in life, it is a huge boost to your confidence. Set small goals regularly and then work hard to accomplish them. Remember, they should be small and reasonable. You can even cut down larger goals into smaller achievable steps. For example, if your goal is to buy a car, you can create a goal to save a certain amount of money by the end of the month, and then every month after that.

Change Small Habits About Yourself

Trying to change a large habit all at once can be very difficult, and the chances of failure are high. This will be a huge shot to your confidence. Instead, focus on smaller habits that will lead to big change. For example, if your goal is to wake up early and workout before starting your day, then don't try to wake up two hours earlier on the first day. Start by waking up 10-20 minutes early until it becomes a habit, and then increase the time from there as you feel comfortable.

Focus Your Attention on Solutions

So often, we are completely focused on the problems and pay no attention to the solutions. For example, you may always complain about being tired, but do nothing to change it, because the solutions never enter your mind. Make it a habit to focus on solutions whenever a problem enters your mind. You will get more accomplished and gain a lot of self-confidence. For example, if you are tired every day, then what is making you that way. Are you not sleeping enough? If not, then why is that? Are you eating too much sugar before going to bed? Do you have a poor diet during the day? Are you drinking enough water? See how man questions you can get answered if you just shift your focus from the problems to the solutions. Try it out with any small problems that you may have and notice the results.

Become Active

You may have noticed that when you start taking action, work starts getting done. So often, people sit around and worry about how they will get something done, rather than doing the work to get it done. Excessive worry leads to a lack of confidence. The more you worry, the lower your self-confidence will become. If you take action, you will obtain results. Results lead to increased confidence. Next time you find yourself worrying about something, start developing a plan and execute it. Hours of taking actions will give you better results than hours of sitting around and worrying.

Gain More Knowledge

Empowering yourself with knowledge is one of the greatest ways to build self-confidence. You will never know everything, but the more you know, the better you will feel about yourself. This goes along the same vein as building competence. You become more knowledgeable on a subject by studying and practicing it. This does not have to be something you will use. It can just be for your own self-fulfillment. According to psychology, one of the biggest reasons for low self-confidence is either misinformation or a lack of information. As you become more empowered with knowledge, you will gain more information too.

Just like with the steps to gain self-esteem, these previous steps must be employed regularly. Our self-confidence will be challenged all the time, so it is in our best interest to build it up regularly through practice and discipline. Think of your confidence as a muscle that you must work out every single day. Do this, and you will be amazed at how much self-confidence you have throughout your life.

Overcoming Procrastination

People love to procrastinate. And why wouldn't they? Why do something now if you can do it tomorrow? I'll tell you why. What keeps you from making the same excuse tomorrow? Also, how do you know what tomorrow will bring? Perhaps something will happen that prevents you from doing the task then, too. A better question to ask yourself is: Why wait until tomorrow if you can get it done now.

Procrastination is a huge problem in our society, and it leads to a lot of anxiety. This anxiety, in turn, leads to a lack of self-confidence. Procrastination is basically a form of being unprepared. Let's say you have a project due on Friday, and it is now Monday. If you begin working on it now, and do a little bit each day, you will have more confidence in completing the project and doing it well, than you would if you started on Thursday. Imagine how much more thorough you can be by starting projects a little bit earlier. The following are a few easy action steps you can take to help overcome procrastination.

- Do not take on more than you can handle. Keep the number of decisions you have to make to a minimum. The more you have to decide on, the more likely you are to procrastinate.

- Begin focusing on the benefits of completing something, rather than the task. For example, if you are working on a project for work, imagine how good it will feel when it's done. Also, think about the rewards that might come if you perform the task well, like a promotion or raise. This focus on the benefits will give you more motivation to get started.

- Prepare yourself for a task by becoming educated on it. Be aware of your limitations before even picking up a new project and do what you can to obtain the necessary knowledge before moving forward. Once again, knowledge will lead to confidence, and confidence makes you active in a pursuit.

- Turn distractions into rewards. If you cannot get your work done because you are always binge-watching shows, then force yourself to turn them into rewards after a hard day's work. For example, set a timer for three hours and use that time to focus on your projects. After the three hours, pat yourself on the back and watch an episode of the show you like. Remember that you have to stay disciplined.

- Set up a daily schedule system for yourself. For example, the first two hours in the morning are designated for the most important tasks, then a break, followed by two hours of the less important tasks, then another break, and finally, dedicating the last part of the day towards the least important tasks. Once you set up a schedule, stick to it to the best of your ability.
- Avoid getting stuck on a project. Give yourself a certain amount of time on a specific task, and if you cannot make progress, move onto something else and revisit it later. There is no sense in wasting time being nonproductive on something.

Follow these steps religiously and watch procrastination be an afterthought in your life.

Build Confidence At Work

Our jobs are a major part of our lives, and it is important to have self-confidence in this environment. We went over building self-confidence in the general sense earlier in this chapter, and now we will focus on more specific areas in our lives. Many of the action steps and techniques are still the same, while some will be more geared towards work.

- Cut out the negative self-talk. Do not beat yourself up at work. It will do nothing for you. Speaking kindly and encouragingly to yourself and you will learn from whatever mistakes you made more easily.

- Boost your knowledge any way you can, and it is a surefire way to achieve confidence. Stay up on the latest research, services, and products within your company and industry as a whole. Imagine being able to bring an idea to your workplace simply because you read up on it. This will make you feel very good about yourself. Always try to stay ahead of the curve.

- Use opportunities to teach others who know less about a subject than you do. Being able to teach others effectively will boot your own knowledge and confidence.

- Practice what you know incessantly, and always look for ways to improve. Identify and correct mistakes along the way.

- Do not speak poorly about others. This already shows a lack of confidence in yourself. When you compliment and speak highly of other people, you acknowledge their strengths and make them feel good about themselves. In turn, you feel good about yourself, too. This also helps to build a nontoxic work environment.

- Pick up new skills to enhance proficiency at your job.

- Ask questions when you do not know something. You may think that you will feel stupid if you ask a question. However, asking and then doing it right, is a bigger boost to confidence than not asking and screwing things up.

- Eliminate negative language, even if it's not geared at anybody. Negative language can affect our psyche on the deepest levels, effectively lowering our confidence levels without us even realizing it.

- Focus on all of the success you have had at work, rather than the failures.

Chapter 4: Getting Rid of Social Anxiety

Social anxiety encompasses many areas of our lives, such as personal relationships, engaging in activities, hanging out in large groups, or giving public speeches. In order to engage in any of these areas, we must overcome our social anxiety, which is essentially having a lack of confidence in social settings. Depending on the individual, social anxiety will either impact them no matter what setting they're, while for others, it will be more selective. For example, a person may be very talkative and confident among his friends but will be terrified when speaking or performing on stage.

This can be the other way around, too. Legendary late-night host, Johnny Carson, was magnanimous on stage but known to be quiet, reserved, and even shy in small groups. We will go over some basic techniques to improve your social anxiety. These will be effective in just about any setting you are in. These techniques are involved with cognitive behavioral therapy, which is a psychologically-based approach to dealing with anxiety, that is drugfree.

- Think about what you're avoiding. As always, the first step in solving a problem is by identifying what it is. What specific social settings are you avoiding. For instance, some people have stated things like using a public restroom, ordering food at a restaurant, becoming scared in a large group, or speaking up at a meeting. Determine what settings cause your social anxiety. Write these down somewhere so you can keep track.

- Now, take your list that you made and develop some type of rating system. This is used to determine the level of anxiety you might experience in each situation to determine what makes it worse. If you feel the most anxious while giving a public speech, then you can rate that as a 10, and then move down from there. So if being around friends gives you none or very little anxiety, that can be a 0 or 1 rating. These ratings are based mainly on predictions. Basically, we are predicting how we would react in certain social settings.

- The next step is to test your predictions. Go out and put yourself in specific situations that may or may not give you the level of anxiety you predicted. For instance, you may have thought you would be at a level of 9 when meeting someone new at a party, but once you did, it was actually around a 4 rating. You may surprise yourself at how well you can actually cope with your anxiety.

- Identify safety behaviors that you use and work to eliminate them. These are superstitious behaviors that people engage in to make them feel safer. I am not talking about carrying a rabbit's foot. Safety behaviors are things like pre-medicating before a social event, avoiding eye contact, rehearsing what you're going to say, or walking with stiff shoulders. The main problem with these types of behaviors is that you will believe they are the only way to get through an anxiety-casing situation. The more you give up these behaviors, the better your experience will be. Imagine how much better a conversation will be when it's natural, rather than scripted.

- Challenge your anxious thoughts. Instead of thinking about how bad things will go, start thinking about how they will go well. If you are worried about looking foolish, ask yourself why that is, and when have you actually looked foolish in the past? Is it real or made up in your head.

- Practice doing what makes you anxious. The classic example here is giving a speech in front of a mirror or recording yourself while you speak alone in your living room. Remind yourself that people don't usually know what your internal feelings are unless you make it obvious to them. This means that no one may have noticed your anxiety in the past. Eventually, test out what you've practiced in the real world. In the case of a speech, after practicing alone for a while, you can perform it in front of some friends.

- Practice self-reward, rather than post-mortem. Post-mortem means that a person analyzes and criticizes every little thing that they've done during a social encounter. If they were standing awkwardly, they become focused on that. Instead, reward yourself for facing the anxiety-causing situation.

Remember to always rinse and repeat with all of these techniques. They must be done regularly until you develop a pattern. You will never be fully confident in every situation. The world will throw things at you that will make you take a few steps back and throw you off your game. That is okay. The key to these exercises is to build up a certain level of self-confidence so that you will be ready to engage and deal with whatever life throws at you. You will develop true strength and knowledge to overcome, no matter how unfamiliar a situation is.

PART III

Chapter 1: Knowing Anger

Anger is a strong feeling. We all despise anger. Yet, none of us is without anger. It is a strong feeling of hostility or displeasure. Like happiness and sorrow, anger is also an emotional state. The state of anger can vary in intensity and expression. Anger could be expressed as mild irritation to a fit of rage or intense fury.

Most people believe anger to be a part of a person's personality. This is an incorrect approach towards anger, and as long as this approach is followed, managing anger would always be incredibly difficult.

You must understand that anger cannot be a part of the character of a person and expressed without reason. However, most of the time, the expression of anger is unreasonable, disproportionate, and undesirable.

Benjamin Franklin once rightly said, 'Anger is never without a reason, but seldom with a good one.

A person who is generally angry from everyone would also have reasons like disappointment, resentment, fear, and other such emotions inside, and the anger just works as a façade to hide a cocktail of such emotions.

Anger as an emotion can be broadly classified into two categories:

1. **Anger as a Primary Emotion:** This is the feeling of anger, irritation, or annoyance originating as a direct consequence of an action or event. This is a response that would originate inside you without a thought. It is

instinctive, unprocessed undiluted, and usually shortlived. If there isn't an escalation event, this anger will dissipate on its own as it is also inconsequential.

>*Example:* Someone driving rashly in front of you or jumping lanes without reason.

2. **Ange as a Secondary Emotion:** Anger as a secondary emotion can be dangerous as it is escalating in nature. Anger comes as a veil to hide other vulnerabilities, and hence it needs to be stronger and effective. Anger as a secondary emotion can be termed as a reaction to other emotions. Those emotions are stronger, more relevant, and forceful, but they remain hidden underground. The structure is similar to an iceberg where the anger is the visible tip that is sharp but may not be very significant in appearance, whereas the underlying emotions or the base of the iceberg can be enormous. Fear, frustration, hurt, rejection, and several other primary emotions can be hiding behind anger.

Secondary emotion can be more dangerous as it can completely overtake your rational thought process. It can get shunted off from the primary emotions and begin working on its own misdirecting you completely.

>*Example:* Road rage is a good example of secondary emotion. You begin an argument due to the frustration of being cut-off by another driver, but it soon gets escalated. Very soon, it doesn't remain about being cut off or not following the traffic rules. Feeling frustrated at being stuck in traffic is another example of anger as a secondary emotion. You feel angry as a

result of your frustration of not being able to go reach somewhere on time.

Understanding Anger

You must understand that anger is a very common emotion. Every person on this earth feels anger. Irrespective of the person's beliefs or faith. However, some people can manage their anger well as they have mastered the art of understanding the cause and its effects. Whereas others are unable to manage their anger well and fall into the vicious trap of actions and reactions.

If you want to learn to manage your anger well, you must know the following things clearly:

1. **Anger** is also an **EMOTION**: Most people are never able to have any control over their anger as they are ashamed of recognizing it. Most of the time, they are simply trying to hide it under the covers. The key to managing your anger issues is to identify and accept anger like other emotions such as love, happiness, and sorrow.

2. **Everyone** Gets **Angry**: This is without exception. No matter who you are talking but you can be sure that the person in question feels anger for sure. It is a common and basic emotion. The only difference is that some people can understand the underlying cause of their anger and deal with the root issues, and others keep fiddling with the effects of the anger. The people who can get to the root cause will be able to deal with the issues more effectively, and hence a more dramatic display of anger wouldn't remain necessary.

3. **Anger** Has **Many Aspects**: What most people don't realize is that anger doesn't necessarily have to be linear. It can have several aspects, and hence there is no need to brush it under the carpet. When we do that, we are trying to get rid of things without understanding them. In this way, the problem doesn't get solved. It stays in its place.

4. **Anger** Can Be **Expressed Differently**: It is common for people to believe that anger can only be expressed explosively. This is besides the fact that most of us express anger in several different ways every day. The day you recognize them and learn to use them in your life, half of the problem would get solved on its own.

Anger is a very strong feeling, and it feeds on our state of mind. The more vulnerable we feel, the stronger the fire of anger would grow, irrespective of our position to express it at that moment or not.

You must understand that there is no way to eliminate anger from the root. The people who talk to acceptance, forget about limits. Anger as an emotion is always inside us. However, it can be both constructive as well as destructive, depending on your control over the djinn called anger. If you understand anger clearly and manage the way you allow it to come out, you'll be doing a great deal of good for yourself as well as for the society.

Management of anger through correct means is not only possible but very much practical. By ignoring anger management issues, you can be straining your relationships with the people around you and also with yourself. It can be constricting, suffocating, and humiliating to deal with your anger silently and dangerous if you let it loose. Anger management techniques can help you in letting it come out in a controlled and calm manner.

Chapter 2: The Physiology and Psychology of Anger

Anger is a major event for the body. When you feel angry and agitated, it is not only your mind that's planning and plotting rapidly but also your body that's readying itself for a fight or flight response that might be needed according to your actions.

Therefore, broadly there are two parts of anger:

The Physiological Impact of Anger

For the body, the angered state rings an alarm bell and activates the sympathetic nervous system. The muscles in the body start tightening up, and it can be termed as a part of the preparation to bear any physical attack.

Anger is also a part of our defense mechanism, and hence the blood pressure in the body rises along with the heart rate. All this is just to enhance the body's ability to react and attack. This mechanism has been designed to enhance our survival rate against a stronger opinion.

You could term the panic attacks as the flight response as that response is generally received when the opponent is undefeatable at that moment. However, anger response is generally fit for situations where you size up to your opponent, or you see a chance of victory. In such circumstances, your sympathetic system increases your heart rate and blood pressure. The hypothalamic nerve cells are also active, and they send messages to the kidneys to work up the adrenal glands. They release large quantities of hormones like cortisol (the stress hormone) the adrenaline, and noradrenaline.

You need to note that the cortisol hormone helps in maintaining the level of blood pressure. Too much cortisol in the bloodstream can even cause high blood pressure levels.

In a crisis, these physical changes help your body in generating more force to defend itself or in launching an offensive. For that part, it can be considered a good thing, and it helped our ancestors. However, persistently high cortisol levels can cause serious bodily harm. First, it will lead to unhealthy blood pressure levels. High blood pressure can cause brain hemorrhages, strokes, and heart disease.

Anger as a part of nature can be destructive as it will cause serious physical as well as mental health issues. Victims of anger management issues are more likely to have stress-related disorders and problems.

The Psychology of Anger

Anger is a very powerful emotion and can be very destructive at times. Anger can make you feel hard, crushed, and humiliated if you are not in a position to react immediately. On the other hand, anger-triggering thoughts, along with feelings of pain, threat, and sense of superiority, can also motivate a person to take aggressive action.

Psychologically, anger does offer a temporary boost of self-esteem and righteousness. Anger is generally a defense mechanism to avoid feeling vulnerable. Most of the time, people do not want to deal with their problems such as low self-esteem, helplessness, and vulnerabilities, and they use anger as a mask to hide these weaknesses.

However, the fact is that anger only masks these weaknesses and doesn't solve them or take them away. It can lead to several social and health problems that we have discussed.

Depression, social anxieties, irrational fears, social avoidance, fears, and complete isolation are some of the common mental issues that many people face due to anger issues.

Chapter 3: Why Anger Management Is So Important

Anger is a malignant force and highly infectious. Your anger will not only eat you from within but also inflame your surrounding. A person with a short temperament and volcanic nature is always a burden for others. Even within the family, a safe distance is maintained from such people as an escape is not an option.

Anger may be a short term reaction to any problem or situation but it has a far-reaching impact emotionally, mentally, physically, spiritually, and biologically. We have discussed in detail the biological and psychological impact of anger on our bodies. Let us look at the ways it affects our bodies mentally, emotionally, and spiritually.

Impact of Anger on Mentality

The most powerful and also the most dangerous thing about anger is that it shuts the logical brain and switches on the survival mode. This means when a person is angry, 'flight or fight' are the only two options in the mind of the victim and there is no process going on for resolving the issue. The mind is just thinking about temporary solutions. Now, this may or may not help the victim in avoiding the problem at hand momentarily, but it would certainly keep the mind occupied for long. Sometimes it passes without notice if the person is not feeling angry very often as the surge of anger would rise and then settle without leaving a long-lasting impact on the mind. However, if a person develops ager issues and starts experiencing the surge of anger with regularity, the mind would remain trapped in planning and plotting about others. The mind would remain riddled with negativity. This can make the mind toxic and highly insecure. This is one of the biggest reasons why anger management is so important.

Impact of Anger on Emotions

One thing that we must never forget that anger is also an emotion, albeit a rather powerful one. When a person fails to manage anger and starts having frequent anger outbursts, it can give way to emotions that may hinder a peaceful life. Problems like increased anxiety, depression, insomnia, and the absence of mental peace are some of the signs that may emerge. Stability and certainty are conducive for emotional health but they get challenged when a person is struggling with frequent anger outbursts. Effective anger management is very important for emotional health.

Impact of Anger on Spirituality

For many, spirituality is not even a subject of consideration. They believe that it is a topic fit for discussion only by the people approaching the end of the road. But, do you know,

- If you are having frequent episodes of anger or hopelessness then you might be suffering from spiritual distress
- Anger leading to anxiety and depression can also be a sign of spiritual distress
- You might also experience trouble sleeping peacefully

Spirituality is not just a subject of discussion at the end of life. We all have a spirit and a conscious. When we are angry, we do things that are not according to our consciousness. This can start hurting us knowingly or unknowingly.

Mark Twain once said, 'Anger is an acid that can do more harm to the vessel in which it is stored than to anything on which it is poured'. This must always be remembered by all who have anger issues of any sort.

Anger management is a must for such people so that they can find mental, emotional, and spiritual peace along with physical and psychological peace.

However, it is a fact that despite all the good advice some people might not pay attention to anger management. It happens with everything in life. People are repeatedly advised to quit smoking but they are unable to do so. They know alcoholism and drugs are deadly but they are unable to come clean. Anyone can overlook or pretend to unsee, but it is important to understand that the problem doesn't go away just because you aren't paying attention to it. The problem is inching closer to its target and getting stronger. The same is the case with anger management.

You can choose to ignore it but that doesn't mean the problem would become less gargantuan. The longer you ignore the anger issues, the deeper it would get imbibed into your nature and harder it would become for you to overcome the problem.

Dangers of Ignoring Anger Management

Ignoring anger management would increase the risk of health issues like heart diseases, strokes, poor immune system, anxiety, depression, and sleeping issues. Your lungs can get affected and it has a very big impact on your overall longevity.

Anger can make a person emotionally weak and volatile. It increases emotional insecurities and your ability to trust others goes down considerably. Anger increases the stress response in its victims and this means that your emotions can escalate easily and even on petty issues.

The University of Washington School of Nursing conducted a study on anger issues in husbands and wives. It found the poor anger management was a major cause of depressive symptoms and health issues in partners. The study found that while it caused women to experience depressive symptoms, it made men experience a large number of health issues.

An Ohio State University also found that people with poor anger management also have poor healing from wounds.

There are numerous studies to prove that anger issues are not just outbursts experienced due to some provocations but they are a symptom that something is wrong inside us and that needs to be managed.

If you or anyone you know is experiencing anger issues, then they must be addressed immediately as they can be the stepping stone for bigger problems in the future.

Chapter 4: Correct Assessment of Your Anger Issues

The generalization or oversimplification of any problem is the first step towards making it unresolvable. We simply state that anger is bad. This is a general statement. This is not to say that any anger is good but then you'd have to devise a mechanism to stop it completely. There is no such mechanism possible for a natural emotion like anger and that is the core of the problem.

The statement 'Anger is Bad' is correct. However, there is no way you can cut it from its root because it is not an action but an emotion. It is coming from inside. A fact that usually gets ignored is that anger at every level is not even visible. Therefore, the correct way to deal with anger is to assess it correctly and then devise ways to deal with it in a correct measure.

All anger is not the same. If the anger is low, you might feel some emotions passing over you and it'd be gone. It doesn't have any long term effect. If the anger is mild, you are just causing harm to yourself. It can make you feel agitated, humiliated, and bad but it isn't expressed and whatever damage occurs stays inside you. However, when it breaches these levels, it can be harmful not only for you but also for the people around it. It is toxic, inflammatory, and exploding. For a better understanding, we can divide anger on a scale of 10.

Scale 1: At this stage, you simply feel irritated by a few things but you are easily able to ignore them. This usually happens when you are sitting with known or unknown people and listening to the things, ideas, and opinions you don't agree with.

Scale 2: You feel highly irritated and anxious but even at this stage you are in a position to think rationally and hence there is no demonstration of anger. This usually happens when you are getting badgered by the constant questioning of young kids or their childish behavior.

Scale 3: This is the stage where you feel irritated to the extent that you start responding sarcastically. You feel agitated but you can still think rationally and hence even at this stage any kind of altercation can be easily avoided. We usually demonstrate this behavior with our friends, family members, and colleagues. It is easily noticeable but not offensive.

Scale 4: This is the exasperation stage. At this stage, you may feel like shouting at the top of your voice and show your irritation and annoyance but you still keep it inside you. This is a laborious process and you may have to sugar coat your voice to hide your annoyance. However, even at this stage, your thought process is clear and in complete control. You can judge correctly.

Scale 5: This is the stage where your anger is visible on your face and in your behavior. Most people are still able to control an outburst of anger. The begin giving the silent treatment or hard looks but remain restrained to these. Their thought process starts getting muddled with angry thoughts but they are still able to control an outburst.

Scale 6: This is the stage of 'flight'. Your anger starts taking control of your mental dexterity. You are not able to push the angry thoughts from your mind and you are constantly thinking of ways to avoid that confrontation as you fear the negative outcome. Clarity of thought becomes questionable at this stage.

Scale 7: This is the stage where you start feeling cornered and the 'fight' response starts to kick in. The biggest problem at this stage is the mind getting hooked on to that angry thought and blocking any other idea. You start feeling tensed and the sense of 'right or wrong' and 'good or bad' starts getting fainter.

Scale 8: At this stage, retaliation becomes a clear plan of action. You want to say or do things that set the scores straight. Your thought process is completely obscured at this level.

Scale 9: At this stage, your angry emotions completely take over your rational thinking brain. Your words and actions are driven by your emotions. You are retaliatory and reactionary. You want to make others have a taste of their own medicine.

Scale 10: As you can imagine, this is the stage where there are no holds barred. You are thinking completely from your emotions and surviving this moment becomes your priority. This is the explosive stage.

Based on this scale, we can divide people into 4 broad categories:
This is a basic division that can help you understand the extent of the problem you'd need to deal with. The categories are self-explanatory from their names.

1. **Emotionally Stable:** If you are a person whose anger remains within the second scale, you are an emotionally stable person who has complete control over the mind and decisions. You have a positive outlook and you can take things in the right direction.
2. **Light Anger Issues:** People generally staying between 2-3 fall in this bracket. However, they know that their anger easily jumps to 5-6. These

are the people who have had anger outbursts of level 9 or 10 a few times in their lives and they clearly understand the demerits.

3. **Volatile Anger Issues:** These are the people who are struggling with their anger. They clearly understand that their anger is usually on a scale of 8-9. They are completely unable to control their rage and it has become their nature. Even little things around them can cause them to explode. Such people can make the environment around them toxic. They can feel the discomfort people feel around them and some even start taking sadistic pleasure in it. Such people may or may not be physically abusive but would take pleasure in verbal abuse. These people need immediate professional help for anger management issues as they are not only causing harm to others but they are also becoming toxic for themselves.

4. **Volcanic Anger Issues:** These are the people who don't look angry or grumpy all the time but they can explode without a moment's notice. They are highly explosive in their behavior and may become physically or verbally abusive even on unexpected things. They become highly unpredictable and they can cause a lot of harm to themselves and also to others.

Chapter 5: Understanding Simple Ways to Manage Anger

It is unhealthy to be angry. Yet, it is a fact that anger is an emotion and we all feel angry in varying degrees. The important thing is to keep this emotion under control. There can be external and internal events that may agitate you or make you feel angry. You cannot have complete control over such events. The important thing is to learn to control your reaction over such events. This is called anger management.

It is very much possible to manage your anger in most circumstances. If you are a person with volatile or volcanic anger issues then you'd also need professional help as your anger issues can take you on a dangerous path and they can be difficult to manage due to years of negligence. However, in others, the anger management process isn't very difficult, it simply requires a lot of practice and discipline. When the rage starts to develop in a person, the first thing that gets distorted is the clear thought process. Your mind gets completely focused on the event and the kind of turmoil it is causing in your mind. This will only lead to further escalation. The way out is to take your mind away from that raging thought and if possible think about the implications and the big picture.

The most important thing is the management of anger as and when it starts to develop. No matter your level of anger issues, if you can manage the ebbing anger in the initial stages, it would be far easier for you to avoid further complications or escalation. The initial management is crucial.

Although you might think that initial management is also the most difficult as very few people can avoid angry outbursts, this is far from being true. Most people are unable to avoid their anger outbursts because they have either never tried anger management properly or they lack practice.

In this chapter, we will learn some of the ways to manage anger better.

Blowing Off the Steam Mentally

Deep Breathing: Deep breathing for many people may not sound to be such an effective tool but what they don't realize is the during the crucial moments when the rage is building inside you, deep breathing is the best and the most effective tool you'll have. People usually misunderstand the process of deep breathing and the purpose it has.

Deep breathing is an exercise to drive the mind away from the thought fueling your rage and focusing it on calming the body and the mind. You must remember that when you are feeling angry it is just not your mind but also your body at work.

For deep breathing, you neither need any equipment nor any preparation. You can do it while sitting in a room full of numerous people and none of them may take notice.

When you feel yourself getting agitated or sense the rage building inside you:

If you are standing try sitting down if possible
If there is no place to sit, please take some support
If you are sitting, please keep your back straight
If possible, close your eyes
If closing your eyes is not possible
Focus your attention at any point in your front

It can be any point, doesn't need to be any specific thing or marking

Now just try to normalize your breathing
We don't realize, but when we are angry
Our breathing rate increases
Just calm your breathing
There is no need to control your breathing
Just bring your focus on the way you are breathing
Notice if you are breathing fast or slow
With your awareness fixed on your breathing
Just try to notice your breath
Observe your breath
Keep breathing normally

Breathe in
Breathe out

Breathe in
Breathe out

Breathe in
Breathe out

Breathe in
Breathe out

Breathe in
Breathe out

Now observe, is your breathing calm now?
Are you still breathing rapidly?

Breathe in
Breathe out

Breathe in
Breathe out

Breathe in
Breathe out

Now, it is time for deep breathing
It is soothing and calming
You'll inhale through your nose
Very slowly
There should be no rush
You need to inhale as much air as possible
Keep breathing in as long as you can
When you feel full
Hold your breath
Keep holding it for a few seconds
Then exhale even slower than you inhaled
Do not rush your breath
Just push out all the air through your mouth

Begin inhaling through your nose
Keep drawing in air steadily
Keep your awareness fixed on the breath

Feel the sensation air makes at your nostrils

Keep sucking in air deeply

There is no rush

Keep your awareness fixed on your breath

Your mind may wander

You may have thoughts

There is no need to worry

There is no need to focus on them

Just keep your awareness glued to your inhalation

When you are full

Stop

You need to hold this breath a little longer

You might feel the pressure building inside you

There is no need to worry

This pressure is good

This pressure is healthy

When you feel unable to hold the breath anymore

Release it through your mouth

Very slowly and calmly

There is no need to rush

Just breath out all the air inside you

Let all the anger, anguish, and pain anguish get out with the breath

Push out all the anger from your gut

Relax!

Repeat the process several times until you start feeling calm and relaxed

Deep breathing is the most effective exercise in anger management that can help you manage even the most aggressive thoughts easily.

Peaceful Mental Imagery: Another effective way to manage your anger is to meditate using peaceful mental imagery. Most people misunderstand meditation as an activity that requires a lot of preparation and planning. They link it directly to spiritual pursuits. However, meditation is an amazing way to calm the mind. Although as opposed to deep breathing, you'd need to sit down for meditation, this is the only preparation you'd need.

Peaceful mental imagery requires you to close your eyes and focus on a happy, joyful, or pleasant thought that's very close to your heart. Deep breathing would help you a lot in focusing your mind on that pleasant thought but the very imagery in your mind would help in calming the aggressive thoughts in your mind.

This is an amazing way to blow the steam building inside you thinking about something that's not going to be pleasant for you or someone else. The easiest and fastest way to do this is to record something pleasant and calming in your voice in your smartphone or any other recording device and play it whenever you feel the need.

Peaceful mental imageries are very helpful in calming the mind and diverting it toward non-toxic actions.

Loving Kindness Meditation: This is a meditation exercise that you can carry out every morning. Loving-kindness meditation is very helpful in all kinds of anger issues. It is helpful for people who have mind anger issues as it helps them in staying positive. The people who have serious anger issues can also benefit from loving-kindness meditation as it motivates them to stay kind and forgiving throughout the day.

Please sit in a comfortable posture.

Keep your hands in your lap with palms facing upwards

Keep your spine erect

Please keep your neck straight

Do not use a neck rest

Now, please close your eyes

It is a simple exercise into kindness and forgiveness
It will fill you with love
You will feel kindness
You will feel gratitude
You will feel peace

It helps in healing wounds
It helps in recovery
It clears the heart of contempt

With your eyes close, remember the people you meet daily
Think of all the faces you see
The familiar faces

The unfamiliar faces
Some faces you remember
Some faces you don't
Some people are kind to you
Some are helpful
Some are recognizable
Some are inconsequential
But, all of them play some role in your life
It is important to remember them
It is important to think of them with gratitude

Breathe in
Breathe Out

Breathe in
Breathe Out

Breathe in
Breathe Out

Now, think of a person who has been very good to you
A person in your present
Or, a person in your past
A friend, a teacher, a parent, sibling, or any other family member
Any person whom you hold in high regard
Think of the love and affection showered by that person
Think of the feelings that come to your mind when you think of that person
Feel that love all over again
Feel that affection

Doesn't it feel good?
Feel the gratitude that arises in your heart

Now say aloud
I feel blessed
I feel loved
I feel nurtured
I feel the affection
I feel calm
I feel the gratitude

Now say aloud
May I keep feeling blessed forever
May I keep feeling loved forever
May I keep feeling nurtured forever
May I keep feeling the affection forever
May I keep Feeling Calm forever
May I keep feeling the gratitude forever

Now return the feeling for that person
May you keep feeling blessed forever
May you keep feeling loved forever
May you keep feeling nurtured forever
May you keep feeling the affection forever
May you keep Feeling Calm forever
May you keep feeling the gratitude forever

Now think of a person who might have helped you recently

A person who might have served you in some way but you don't know that person well

It can be a clerk in an office

A person driving the cab you took

A waiter who might have served you recently

It can be any person of that sort

Now think of that person

Think of the smile that person had

Think of the service that person gave you that you still remember that person

That person helped you or served you

Form a picture of that person at the back of your mind

Now say aloud

Thank you for your service

Thank you for your kindness

Thank you for your help

Thank you for being nice to me

May you feel blessed

May you feel calm

May you feel loved

May you feel nurtured

May you feel the affection

May you feel the gratitude

May you prosper

May you get happiness and joy

May you achieve all you want

Repeat this a few times

Now, think of a person you do not like
A person who may have been rude to you
A person who spoils your day
A person you may encounter even today
A person you don't like

There is no reason to hold a grudge
There is no reason to hate
There is no reason to be unhappy
It is easy to forgive
It is easy to forget the bad things in the past

Just say aloud,
I forgive you
May you also forgive me
May you feel blessed
May you feel loved
May you be happy
May you also prosper
May your life be filled with joy and prosperity
May you get all you wish for

May you feel my love
May you feel my gratitude
May you feel lots of joy in your life

May you stay healthy

Repeat these lines a few times

Now send out your love to everyone in the world
May all feel loved
May all be blessed
May all be happy
May all beings prosper
May all achieve their goals

Repeat these lines a few times

Keep breathing normally
Breathe in
Breathe out

Breathe in
Breathe out

Breathe in

Breathe out

You can open your eyes when you are ready.

Blowing Off the Steam Physically

Sometimes the anger is very high and you start feeling highly agitated. These are the times when some people find it very hard to focus. At such times, it is better to give a physical release to anger. However, the physical release must come in the right way and under the right conditions. It must not be released in front of others and you must also ensure that no harm comes to you or others in any manner.

Pillow Punching: This is an easy and safe way to release your anger physically. If you are feeling highly agitated and you are unable to control your anger, you can punch your pillow to give your anger a physical release. You must do this only in seclusion and never on other things as it can even cause injury.

Shouting It Out: Shouting out is also a good way to blow out some steam. You can find someplace where no one can hear you or sit in the car with the windows closed and shout out the anger building inside you. This is much better than shouting at someone that can create a nasty scene. It can be very helpful in stressful situations as most of the negative emotions and energies get a proper release.

Power Punching: This is similar to pillow punching with the only difference being the replacement of a punching bag in place of a pillow. Power punching helps you in giving a powerful release to all your anger and it makes you feel relaxed. People generally feel much calmer after they have done some power punching.

Chapter 6: Mindfulness and Anger Management

The Way to Seek Happiness, Inculcate Compassion, Gain Control of Emotions, and Channelize Anger Positively

For the uninitiated, mindfulness can be a difficult thing to understand. It is the practice of being fully present at the moment. This might sound so easy and simple, yet it has become so difficult to practice these days.

'Living in the Moment' is just not the motto of mindfulness but the whole and only principle.

Contemplation of the past and the worries of the future are the biggest causes of all kinds of stress in the world. The more you worry about them, the more worried, stressed, helpless, desperate, and agitated you'll feel. Not only this, worrying about the past and future also takes your focus away from the present where your life currently is. The simple principle of mindfulness helps you only on focusing on your present and letting the past and future be. The most difficult task in mindfulness is the art of letting go, and it will be the only challenge you'll face.

Mindfulness is the practice of keeping the mind calm and relaxed. When the mind is without the fear of the future and the agony of the past, it will react to things in the present normally. It is the practice of living every moment with joy and complete attention, and within this lies the answer to your anger. When your complete focus is on living every moment in the present, and you are rationalizing everything, you stop reacting to things instinctively, and the whole problem of anger lies there.

Mindfulness Is the Practice of Being Aware

These are the times complicating even the simplest of things in life. Mindfulness is not a concept that should cause any kind of confusion. It is the simple art of being aware.

You need to be aware of every thought you have, every action you take, every decision you make, and you stop doing things in an auto-operated mode.

Mindfulness is the art of experiencing everything as a novel and complete experience. Even if you are drinking water, the experience should be immersive. You must feel the taste of water, the way it feels as it quenches your thirst, and the gratitude for the satiation it brings. Being aware of the whole experience is the art of mindfulness.

The only thing you need to be mindfulness is the simple art of paying attention. Now in this age of the internet, where the attention span of the millennials is just 12 seconds and the attention span of young ones in Gen Z is a paltry 8 seconds. Not only this, even within this fickle span of 8 seconds, but the Gen Z is also toggling between several windows. In such a scenario, it is very usual to sacrifice experiences and rely on automated information and reflexes, and that is the basis of the whole problem.

Mindfulness can help you in getting over this problem by encouraging you and giving you the right conditions to pay more attention to experiences and less value to memories and perceptions. Mindfulness teaches you the science of living in reality and staying away from perceived threats and memories. It helps you in living a real life.

For most people, this might sound a very difficult task to perform, and they are not to be blamed for that. Our lives have become so reliant of spoon-fed information and prejudices that even the thought of sensing everything paying attention to detail starts seeming like a tough task.

However, the beauty of mindfulness practice lies in the fact that it gives you the time to learn to enjoy these experiences. You can be practicing the first part of the process, and still, you'll be able to enjoy the process completely.

Four Important Principles in Mindfulness

Non-judgmental attitude: Judgmental attitude is among the most important reasons for increasing anger in society. We are quick to judge and label things as good or bad, right or wrong, or useful or useless. Such judgments come without a complete, fair, or thorough assessment of the object or person. This segmentation creates divides and stereotypes. We all are victims of such divisions and want a break for ourselves. Such divisions lead to anger, unrest, and inequalities. We all want freedom from such unfair divisions; however, when it comes to us, we don't mind following the stereotypes in our minds. Mindfulness helps in breaking such norms to allow you to a life where you don't judge others or get judged by them. Things don't get classified as good or bad. In mindfulness, every experience is just an experience. There is no need to record or memorize that moment for future needs.

Acceptance of Every Experience: Another big reason for the anger inside is our reluctance to accept fears, phobias, worries, inhibitions, weaknesses, guilts, indulgences, greeds, and other such things. We always try to remain free of every negative experience and then live in their fear for the rest of our lives. Mindfulness helps you in accepting every experience in life without any prejudice or fear. It helps you in experiencing and accepting the totality of every experience, thought, and feeling without taking into consideration the fact that they might be good, bad, or neutral.

Readiness to Sense: Another major roadblock in the path of anger management is our stubbornness to stick to the given patterns. We are not ready to feel anything new. We are unable to classify any new experience because we are simply looking for the non-existent set parameters. Mindfulness helps you in learning the art to approach everything with an openness to sense it in its entirety.

Being Aware or Moving with Consciousness: Consciousness or awareness are highly misused words these days. People simply keep using them generically even when they don't mean anything related to them. The words are very clear in themselves. Awareness or the state of being aware simply means having complete knowledge of the things happening around you. We live with the misconception that we are aware, yet most of us can't tell the pleasure of breathing or taking a deep breath inside. This is a basic act that we perform 24X7. Yet, very few people may have felt the sensation air makes as it enters the nostrils. This is a reason very few people think before they begin to react to anger. For managing anger effectively, the most important thing to learn is to become aware of the emotions in your mind. It is an act of being conscious of every thought crossing your mind or consciously, only allowing selective thoughts to proceed.

This is the way mindfulness can help you in managing anger effectively.

Chapter 7: 8-Week Anger Alleviation Plan

It is time to put your full understanding of anger and mindfulness into action. We understand that anger doesn't come from outside. It is an emotion that's inside us and comes out as a reaction. For every reaction, there needs to be a thought. Every thought originates in the mind. If you are mindful and you pay attention to every thought and reaction you give, managing anger would become very easy for you.

In this chapter, we will practice becoming mindful in our practice in 8-weeks. You must keep in mind that being mindful is a lifelong practice. The Buddhist masters following the Zen tradition of meditation practice mindfulness in every act they perform, and yet they can't be certain that they have achieved the desired perfection. Therefore, keeping the art of mindfulness in practice and making it a way of life is the best way to manage your anger through mindfulness.

Week 1

Ditching the Autopilot

As we have discussed at length till now, we all are living our lives on autopilot with no active control over our choices, desires, feelings, emotions, reactions, and experiences. This week, you must stop paying attention to what you know and pay attention to what you can discover and learn.

Simple acts like drinking water or breathing deep can be eye-opening experiences if you perform them with complete awareness. As an experiment, you should start performing deep breathing and chanting a positive affirmation.

This week, your complete focus must remain on doing everything with complete inclusiveness in the task. You must pay attention to every activity. If you are walking, you must be completely immersed in the act.

Week 2

Learning to Sense and Feel to Become Aware

Sensing is the second part of becoming aware. A big problem with the current age is that we are devoid of experiences. The world is full of critics, bloggers, vloggers, and reviewers who tell us about their experience of the things we want to enjoy. They enjoy those things and give us their views, which later on become our views, opinions, and experiences about those things. This is irrespective of the thought that we may have never seen those things or met those reviewers.

The biggest disadvantage of these things is that we are devoided of our own experience. If we read a negative google review about a food joint, not only our opinion changes, we might even not like the food irrespective of the taste it has to offer. It isn't the food but the rating that got rated by our mind, and it got precedence.

In the second week of mindfulness, you'll learn the art of feeling everything and experiencing every taste without judgment. This week, you must learn to feel everything through your senses.

If you are eating something, then you must identify that taste though your senses. The flavors it has and the way it tastes.

Week 3

Meditation and Exercise

In the third week, you must begin practicing meditation and exercises. Simple meditations and exercises will help you in not only becoming aware of the sensations outside, but they'll also help you in understanding your mind and thought process.

Meditation helps you in exploring your mind and your thought process.

In the beginning, you just need to sit in a cross-legged posture and focus on your thoughts. Try to look at the thoughts forming in your mind. Don't try to push any thought aside or intervene. Simply observe the process through which thoughts originate in your mind.

This is a very crucial step in the process of anger management as it helps you understand the basic process of thought processes. The better you'll know your thoughts and the way they form, the easier it'd get for you to manage your thoughts and emotions, and they'll lose power on you.

Practicing simple Yoga steps or other breathing exercises will be great this week. You must practice deep breathing asanas for several minutes a day as they help you in peering deep inside your mind. The deeper you focus on your breath, the easier it would become for you to stabilize your thoughts.

Week 4

Learning to Recognize Negative Thoughts and Mindful Walking

Once you have learned to peer into your mind and the thought process, you must identify the pattern of your negative thought process. In this week, you must learn to label your thoughts correctly and the way a thought begins and matures.

Understanding of negative thought patterns is very important in anger management as they play a key role in exciting and provoking you.
You should observe the thoughts very carefully and then follow their progression. There is no need for you to interrupt them or change their course. Even at this point, your objective should be to understand the way a simple thought turns into a colony of negative thoughts.

You should also begin expanding your area of attention, and mindful walking can be a very good step in this direction. Pacing up and down the room is an activity that most people carry out when they are lost in their thoughts. However, this is very different.

In mindful walking, you need to keep your complete attention on your walking. The way you raise your steps. The way it feels under the palm of your feet. The weight you feel on your legs. All your thoughts exclusively need to be about walking and the experience you are having.

This process helps you in understanding the way you can eliminate thoughts even when you are working.

Week 5

Allowing Things to Be- Without Reacting Impulsively
This week, you'll learn to accept and acknowledge things without reacting to them. Avoidance of negative thoughts and escapism must be eliminated.

You must learn to accept every fact that comes in front of you as just a fact. You must not attach any significance to the thoughts or the facts. It is our habit of attaching significance that leads to problems. We attach a feeling and then make it significant enough to evoke an emotion that eventually gets expressed as anger.

Throughout the week, you will simply acknowledge the facts that come and then allow them to pass without judging them or attaching unwanted significance to them.

Week 6

Every Thought Is Just a Thought

This week is also an extension of the previous week, with the exception being that you'll follow the thought in your mind without attaching any significance to it.

This is the week to learn that every thought is just a thought. It is your mind that makes it scary or fun. A piece of news that might be heartbreaking for you may not mean anything for someone else. Its significance lies in the fact that you gave that news importance and emotion.

If you learn to label every thought just as a thought, managing anger would become very simple for you.

You must think of every negative thing that scared you until now and let it pass through your mind. You must allow it to pass through your mind in your complete awareness so that it loses its ability to scare you forever.

At this stage, your aversion to certain thoughts and ideas must come to an end.

Week 7

Learn to Be Kind to Yourself and Others

This is the week where you must learn to be kind to yourself and others. Practice Loving-Kindness Meditation in the morning and before going to bed at night. Learn to appreciate yourself and others at every step of life. Even if the task is not very big, learn to appreciate the effort and the things that have been done.

The more appreciative you become of yourself and others, the more difficult it would become for you to cultivate anger in your mind.

Practice this throughout the week.

Week 8

Becoming Mindful in Your Routine

This is the week of practicing your mindfulness routine with complete exposure. You don't have to be selective, and neither you have to be perfect. Cultivation of Mindfulness is a lifelong process, and it'd take a much longer practice than the short duration of a few weeks.

However, every journey starts with the first step, and you can consider these 8 weeks as your stepping stones into the amazing world of anger management through mindfulness.

PART IV

Chapter 1: Back to the Basics

When most people think of mindfulness, they envision monks or yogis, sitting cross legged for hours with closed eyes and poised fingers overlooking the Himalayas. Although mindfulness is present in the lives of monks and yogis, what most people don't know is how easy it is to incorporate mindfulness into our everyday lives. As a matter of fact, a mindful state is the most natural and restful state for human beings—a state in which we were all living and moving in as children. If you think back to your childhood, you will likely remember that your concept of time and perception of reality was much different. Most children are very in touch with their emotions, letting them come and go naturally. If a child falls down in one moment and skins their knee, the child will likely begin to cry. However, if a few moments later they are being offered ice cream, their tears will dry, and they will continue on with their day. Mindfulness is the reason children are so in tune with the details of life that adults seem to miss. It is also the reason they are more likely to screech with joy, run around excitedly in enjoyable environments, wake up easily in the morning, and take the time they need to calm down from anger or sadness until the next happy moment arises. Children spend very little time thinking about things beyond the present moment. Even if they have something to look forward to, they are still likely to become invested in the moment at hand, whether that is playing, enjoying time with their parents, or eating a meal. So, what happens as people grow older that brings us away from this natural state of mindfulness?

There are a number of factors that pull people out of the present moment. From the time a child begins elementary school, they are presented with a schedule for the day, which remains relatively the same. Children are expected to remain within the structures presented to them, and the idea of forward-thinking and preparing for the next hour's activity becomes introduced. As they grow, children will likely have more expectations placed upon them, whether those expectations are academic, extracurricular, or within the home. Of course, it is necessary for children to learn how to be responsible and dedicate the time they need to the important things in life. However, as they become further exposed to the constant rush and future-oriented thinking of their parents and teachers, they come to see time as something that no longer belongs to them to fully inhabit.

Furthermore, as people approach teenage and young adulthood, they will begin to face challenges that most children are either shielded from or otherwise unaware of. People become flooded with the pressure to perform well and always be doing more today than yesterday. Although the expectations of cultures and societies vary, we can be sure that people are overwhelmed with the pressure to meet those expectations in order to be considered successful and valid. Once one bar is crossed, another one is waiting, and there is no time to slack. Additionally, the older people become, the more likely they are to be subject to long-lasting pain in their lives. This can come in the form of relationships ending, failing to accomplish something, being mistreated by other people, losing and grieving loved ones, or coming to terms with painful childhood events that did not make sense at the time. Teenagers become increasingly subject to mental health issues as they advance into adulthood, having to face all of the hard realities of the world and still come out on top. People may also be subject to trauma as a result of illness, accident, or abuse. All of these factors are enough to work against people and pull them out of the present moment, either because it is too painful to be there, or because they are simply too distracted.

Human beings experience over 60,000 thoughts per day, but the vast majority are dedicated either to planning for the future or worrying about the past. Becoming overly concerned about the future or steeping in the pains or regrets of the past can increase levels of stress in the body, which makes people more anxious and prone to physical health problems.

The mind naturally wanders, and it is impossible to keep thoughts from coming. Mindfulness is not a tool to eradicate such thoughts, as is the common misconception. Rather, it is a tool through which to acknowledge the thoughts the mind creates, bring attention to them, and allow them to move through. This ultimately brings people into what is happening here and now and gives them more control over their minds and how they orient themselves in their environments.

Because mindfulness is a skill that all human beings are equipped with at our core, it is something that can be re-learned. Just as we exercise our bodies to strengthen our muscles, so we must work to strengthen our brain through mindfulness. The way this strengthening happens is through being aware of thoughts as they arise, then breathing back into the present moment. The more practice is given to returning to the present moment, the stronger the mind will become in remaining in the present more often. Just as the body physically strengthens and becomes healthier over time with exercise, mindfulness exercises can physically change the structure of the brain to make it healthier. Mindfulness activates the positive components of the hippocampus, which is the part of the brain responsible for good things like creativity, joy, and the ability to process emotions. This, in turn, decreases stress levels, depressive tendencies, addictive behaviors, and the fight or flight instinct by shrinking the part of the brain responsible for negative things (the amygdala). Overall, increased mindfulness is the key to a longer, healthier, more creative, and more joyful life.

Chapter 2: Unlocking Your True Purpose Through Mindfulness

Re-centering Yourself

Everyone has days where everything seems to be spinning out of control, and there seems to be no way to manage the chaos. The days where you wake up late, run late to work, spill coffee on your shirt, get cut off on the road, get yelled at by your boss, spend the entire day at work in a confused frenzy, only to come home and bicker with your partner. Since the beginning of time, the human mind has been conditioned to release stress hormones and illicit the fight or flight instinct for the purpose of protection and survival. In the past, this primal instinct was very useful for escaping threats. As times have changed, the threats have become less severe, but the brain's response has remained largely the same. Now, these fight or flight reactions are likely to be triggered by everyday scenarios, such as those previously detailed. The hormone-induced responses that occur when we're stressed out are quick to send us spiraling into emotionally dramatic, and far less peaceful dimensions.

The good news is, mindfulness can be used as a tool for re-centering and gaining control over your anxiety and emotional reactions when you start to feel yourself spiral. Although there is no way to avoid stress and drama in daily life, mindfulness can serve as a shield of calm presence to protect your well-being. If you are preparing to enter a situation that you anticipate could be stressful, like a high-stakes day at work, a scary doctor's appointment, or a difficult conversation with a loved one, it can be incredibly helpful to bring yourself down to a more calm and balanced state in preparation for the stress you are about to deal with. You may find yourself with a racing heart, sweating palms, an unclear head, and the feeling of "butterflies in your stomach." Another area where it is common to feel these physical effects of anxiety is when encountering dramatic situations. Drama can arise tense moments with other people, as well as within the theoretical situations people create for themselves when worrying about what they cannot control (for example, the perception other people have of them, or events that may or may not occur in the future). Giving attention to what is happening in your mind and body and allowing yourself to breathe into the moment can be a total lifesaver in moments of drama or stress. Two to three minutes of deep breathing in your car before going to work, or taking a few deep breaths before reacting in a tense moment, can make a drastic difference in your sense of balance and your ability to deal with stress without launching into fight or flight.

Giving Your Emotions Space

The goal of mindfulness is not to eliminate emotions, but rather, to gain control over the impact they have on how we orient ourselves in the world. It is vital to honor our emotions and give them space to exist and teach us, without letting them seize control. Mindfulness is an excellent tool for giving our emotions space in this way. When an emotion arises, mindfulness gives us a chance to observe that emotion without judgment. In this calm space, we can ask our emotions, "What are you trying to teach me?" We can more clearly discern why we are experiencing a certain emotion, and become in touch with the deeper needs that may have caused that emotion to arise. Just as a child may cry when they need to be nourished our held, we may find ourselves growing angry or agitated when we need support, touch, or self-care. Similarly, we may find ourselves feeling stressed or anxious in scenarios that are subconsciously triggering moments from the past. In these cases, our stress and anxiety are begging us to become in touch with our past self, reminding ourselves that we are safe, and the traumatic moments from the past are over. Once our emotions have been given a non-judgmental space to exist, they can smoothly and peacefully move through the body and be released. This frees us to move from moment to moment like children do, without being constrained by unresolved emotions. Additionally, giving this space to our emotions in mindfulness helps to temper our reactions, which can prevent us from acting out in extreme ways and potentially doing or saying something we regret.

Making Clear Decisions

With the human mind constantly being muddled with thoughts, it can be hard to see things clearly. Sometimes our minds are cluttered by the expectations flying at us from every different direction, or perhaps by our fears of what will happen if things don't go to plan. When it comes to making decisions, we are often faced with numerous options, and it can be difficult to navigate through the chaos in our minds to come to a well thought out resolution. In a distracted, anxious, or removed state, our minds are like a pond on a rainy day—rippling to a point where there is no more clarity. Mindfulness is the calming of the waters, which brings us to a place where we can more clearly think of all possible outcomes of a decision and check in with what we truly need before moving into the next moment.

Keeping Yourself Safe

Although fight or flight instincts originally developed as a way to keep humans safe, in many modern-day scenarios, they do quite the opposite. Let's go back to the example from the beginning of the chapter about the chain of events in a typical chaotic day. If you wake up late in the morning and rush to make your coffee, not paying attention to what you are doing, you run the risk of haphazardly screwing the lid on your to-go cup, then sloshing boiling hot coffee over the edge of the cup and onto yourself as you bolt out the door. Although such a scenario could simply result in a stained shirt, the inattentiveness could have a more drastic effect, such as burning yourself or someone else. Driving to work in a state of panic over running late causes you to be more likely to break the rules of the road—driving too fast, making dangerous decisions when changing lanes, taking turns too fast, running yellow lights just before they turn red, etc. Additionally, the panicked state can lead to anger with yourself or others on the road, which can further impair judgment and put you at greater risk of an accident. Attempting to have a conversation with your boss if you are in fight or flight mode could result in being overly emotional and saying or doing something extreme which could place you at odds within your workplace, potentially even costing your position. Going throughout your day in a frenzy causes you to be less aware of what is going on around you, which can lead to further threats to safety like leaving a burner on, forgetting to eat or drink enough water, or neglecting those in your care (such as pets or children) as a result of your own inner distractions. Finally, as stress from the day carries into the home at the end of the day, it can pose a major threat to relationships. The more stressed out and less clear thinking you are, the more likely you are to say or do something threatening to your partner, to put yourself in an aggressive and volatile situation, and to make brash decisions that have the potential to haunt your future.

Improving Relationships

Just as we must give ourselves space to learn, grow, and process our experiences, we must give that space to those around us as well. When a partner or friend is acting in a way we don't enjoy, mindfulness can allow us to take a step back and look at the situation from a position of empathy. We can allow ourselves to hold space for whatever that person may be going through individually and express our support while also maintaining boundaries and staying in control of what we can. Everyone is deserving of space to be listened to, understood, and supported for who they are. However, it is incredibly difficult to give that space to anyone if it has not been cleared within oneself.

When we operate out of a mindless state, there is hardly any space to meet our own needs and process our own experience, much less to provide that to other people. This can lead us to be closed off to the ones we love, push them away, or act out in anger, selfishness, or aggression. If we have not given space to what is going on within us, we cannot offer full empathy to others. Only 20% of the population is recorded to practice true empathy, which can be linked to the rarity of true mindfulness among adults. Mindfulness allows us to be more present to our own needs in order to hold adequate space for the needs of others as well.

Attention and mutual respect are core elements of every functional relationship. Practicing mindfulness can improve relationships with all the people in our lives by preparing us for every engagement and calming our minds enough to be fully present in the moments we share with others. Mindfulness clears the space for us to listen intentionally to other people and pay more attention to what kind of people they are and what kind of support they need. It allows us to love other people better by increasing our awareness of how they feel most loved. By being present in the moment at hand, as opposed to trapped in the past or future, you are more likely to remember to pick up the phone and give your grandmother a call, to be fully engaged when interacting with your child, or to remember the kind of kombucha your significant other likes best from the store. Not only does mindfulness allow for more meaningful conversations and joyful memories, but it also increases the functionality of our relationships overall so that both ourselves and those we love are feeling fully respected, listened to, and encouraged.

Fostering True Joy

We often hear the term "childlike joy" to describe moments of pure bliss, enthusiasm, and full satisfaction. As people grow into adults, such moments tend to be few and far between, with many remembering the most joyful moments to have been those that occurred in childhood. The expectations of daily life become too much, and most people find themselves trapped in a cycle of constant anticipation. People spend so much time thinking about where they would rather be (on vacation, in bed, enjoying the weekend) that the days melt into each other without us realizing all the moments of our lives we are missing. The biggest societal misconception is that true happiness lies in what we do not yet have. We are flooded with lies such as "Once I can buy this new TV, then I'll be happy," or, "Once I have a partner, then I'll be happy," or, "I'll be happy once I can say I've been to five different countries." Mindfulness abolishes these lies by proving to us that the capacity for true joy lies not in the future but in the here and now. Wherever you are right now, whatever you have, and whichever stage of life you're in, mindfulness reminds you that *this* is your chance to experience beauty and satisfaction like never before. Take time to look at the flowers you did not notice growing in front of your neighbor's house, the complexity of coffee's flavor as it slides down your throat, the way your loved one's eyes crinkle when they smile, the laughter of a child, every intricate flavor of dinner, or the unique people wandering up and down the streets you drive every day to work. It is here that joy resides; all you have to do is be present enough to recognize it.

Chapter 3: Moving Mindfully in Daily Life

Coming to the Present Moment: Daily Guided Mindfulness Meditation With Journaling (Week 1)

Cultivating Mindfulness

This meditation should be done in a space where you feel fully comfortable, safe, and relaxed. Perhaps it is in a corner of your bedroom, in a garden, by your favorite lake, or even in your car. Make sure you can fully relax and avoid distractions. Some people meditate best with instrumental music or nature sounds in the background, while others prefer silence. Feel free to try multiple methods and see which is most soothing to you (this can vary depending on the day). You may do this meditation sitting in a chair, on a mat, or lying flat on your back with your palms up to the sky. You will need to give yourself 5-20 minutes of time to practice, depending on your skill level and current state. If you like, you can set a timer.

Start by coming into the moment with a few deep breaths. Settle into your body and take note of any sensations you feel. If you feel pain, tingling, warmth, or tightness in any part of your body, focus your breath into that space. Imagine any tension unfurling into openness. Notice as your thoughts arise. Take notice of them, then allow them to pass as you come back to the breath. If it is helpful, you can try a breathing pattern in order to culminate focus. To do the 4-4-4 breathing pattern, breathe in for 4 counts, hold for 4 counts, and breathe out for 4 counts. To do the 5-5-7 breathing pattern, breath in for 5 counts, hold for 5 counts, release for 7 counts. Sometimes it helps to imagine breathing in the things you wish to see more of in your daily life (creativity, love, patience, openness) and exhale the negative things (fear, negativity, sadness, stress). Allow yourself to spend a few moments in a more active state of breathing in, releasing, and paying attention to your body.

With practice, you may enter a state where your thoughts slow and you become fully grounded in the present moment. In this state, you are no longer bombarded with thoughts, nor distracted by elements of your environment. It becomes easier to return to the breath. All restlessness and tension in the body seem to melt away, and the mind reaches a flowing, liquified state. There may be days when you cannot enter into this state, and you remain restless throughout the course of the meditation. If this happens, allow it to be that way, observing every thought that arises, then letting it go.

After the time is up, begin to arrive in the moment by moving your body slightly—wiggling your fingers and toes, tensing and releasing your muscles, etc. Next, you're your eyes. Notice how bright and clear the world looks to mindful eyes. Notice the calm, transcendent feeling in your body, and continue to move with it as you go about your day.

Mindfulness Meditation Journal Prompt (Week 1):

What did you feel in your body before beginning? What do you feel now?

Which thoughts continued to arise in your consciousness? Could these thoughts have been trying to teach you something or speak to a deeper need you may have?

How does the world look after opening your eyes? What do you notice?

Come back after going about your day for several hours. Did you bring mindfulness with you into the world? If so, how?

Coming to the Present Moment: Daily Guided Mindfulness Meditation With Journaling (Week 2)

Taking Mindfulness Into the World

This meditation will be done with your eyes open in moments if your daily life. This is not a specific meditation you have to set aside time for, but rather a state you come into. Notice where your attention goes in a given moment. If your attention is drawn to a particular sight, like the nearest tree or a view from the top of a mountain, allow yourself to see it fully. Repeatedly tell yourself, "see, see, see." Breathe as you allow your eyes to truly become totally focused and take in the image fully, allowing it to become a part of your awareness.

If your attention is drawn to an auditory experience, such as the sound of cars on a city street, a rushing body of water, or an internal monologue, give full attention to that thing. Soak in that auditory experience, breathing slowly and telling yourself, "hear, hear, hear."

You may also be drawn to a particular physical or emotional experience within the body. This experience may be positive, like a pleasant bodily sensation or a feeling of joy. It may also be negative, like physical pain, or feelings of anger or feel. Either way, allow yourself to become fully present with what is there, breathing into the experience and seeing what it has to teach you. Breathe into that bodily experience, telling yourself, "feel, feel, feel."

Throughout the day, you'll find that your attention is pulled in various directions. Mindfulness is the choice to tune in to whichever place you're going in a given moment and give full attention to that experience for whatever it is.

Mindfulness Meditation Journal Prompt (Week 2):

How difficult was it to bring mindfulness into your daily life in this way? Where did you face the most challenges?

Did your attention tend towards certain experiences (visual, auditory, bodily) more than others?

Describe a specific moment where you brought mindfulness to your experience and felt truly present. What did you observe?

Coming to the Present Moment: Daily Guided Mindfulness Meditation With Journaling (Week 3)

Mindfulness at Work (or School)

The first part of this meditation should happen in a place outside of work, where you feel safe, calm, and separated from the issues you may face in the workplace. Start by identifying your biggest struggles at work. The journal portion will give you a space to write them down. Do you struggle with productivity? Boredom? Stress? Conflict resolution? Work relationships? Once you have identified your most significant area(s) of struggle, close your eyes and visualize what that unpleasant experience looks like. Perhaps it looks like you, rushing around mindlessly like a bee in a hive, stressed out and too overbooked to step away and breathe because there are more calls to make, more e-mails to send, more things to do. Or, perhaps it is the co-worker, professor, or boss that makes your stomach drop whenever you think about having to interact with them. Perhaps you feel unfulfilled at work and find yourself constantly checking the clock, thinking about the moment you get to leave. Maybe you have so many things to do and no idea where to start, so you waste a lot of time on mindless tasks. Whatever your struggles at work are, use your time and space away from work to safely visualize the situation. Breathe into the mental circumstance.

As you breathe, begin to envision what this experience would look like if it went the way you want it to. Perhaps it looks like the mental clarity that allows you to know exactly what needs to get done and how to make the best possible use of your time. It could be a greater sense of calm and courage when talking with your difficult boss or co-worker and having your message be well-received on their end. It may also be a deeper sense of satisfaction and enjoyment in the work you're doing, providing you the ability to step back and feel a sense of joy with where you're at, without constantly thinking about the next thing. Reframe the moment in your mind until you've created a mental space that feels good. Let yourself sit there, breathing, soaking it in for several minutes.

Once you go into the workplace (or school), you can bring this meditation into your life by going back to the peaceful mental image you've created over and over again. When you begin to feel stressed, bored, anxious, or unproductive, return to the space where you do not feel those things. Bring that energy into your daily work life, and watch how it revolutionizes your experience.

Mindfulness Meditation Journal Prompt (Week 3):

What do you identify as your biggest challenge(s) at work or school?

How does it look when you reframe your struggles to create a positive mental image?

What do you observe about bringing this positive mental image into difficult situations in the workplace or at school?

Mini Meditation Toolbox: 15 Quick and Easy Meditations to Integrate Mindfulness Into Your Daily Life

One-Minute Mindfulness

- Find a space where you can be alone, like on your bathroom break or in your car right before going into work, school, or home at the end of the day.
- Set a timer for one minute
- Close your eyes and focus exclusively on your breathing
- Take notice of the stresses, thoughts, and anxieties that arise, then let them go
- When you open your eyes, notice how you feel de-stressed, clear-minded, and prepared to go about your upcoming tasks and interactions with others

5-Minute Body Scan

- Set a timer for 5 minutes (if needed)
- Close your eyes and take several deep, cleansing breaths. You may use the 4-4-4 or 5-5-7 breathing patterns to deepen the breath
- Begin to bring attention to your body
- Take notice of any sensations that arise-- warmth, tingling, tension, etc.
- Bring your attention to the soles of the feet. Tighten your muscles by curling your toes, then release. What sensations do you feel?

- Continue moving up the body to your calves, hips, abdomen, chest, hands, arms, face, and neck. Observe any sensations that arise, and breathe into those sensations.
- Tighten and release the muscles in each of these areas, allowing any pent-up energy or resistance to be released
- Feel your body become grounded, relaxing completely into the floor, bed, or chair as you come into the present moment in your body and all tension melts away

Mindful Bath/Shower (10-minute meditation)

- As you begin your bath or shower, take a moment to breathe. Remove yourself from the stresses of the day and allow yourself to re-center
- Bring attention to each part of your body as you wash it
- Take notice of any sensations you feel as you move from the soles of your feet to the ends of your hair
- Breathe in the pleasant scent of the soaps and the warmth of the water. Allow yourself to feel clean, warm, and safe.
- As you wash each part of your body, thank it for what it does for you. Then, thank yourself for taking care of your body.

Mindful Morning Routine (15-30 minutes)

- Before getting out of bed, begin to stretch gently, letting thoughts come and go as your mind and body wake up. Do not rush yourself.
- Once you are ready to get out of bed, bring your attention to the space around you and the day ahead. Feel yourself become fully present in that space and prepared to move mindfully through your day
- Pay attention to every move you make, from putting on clothes, to washing your face, to setting the water on the stove to boil.
- Cultivate your awareness for the day ahead by moving slowly and calmly, one task at a time, becoming fully awake to the world

Mindful Housekeeping
- Allow yourself to become focused on the task at hand and only that task. Let every other thing you have to do or think about fade into the background.
- Bring your attention to the breath and the specific way your body moves as you complete a particular task or chore
- Give space to any thoughts or emotions that arise in your consciousness, allowing yourself to process them in a mindful state

Mindful Sit-and-Drink (10-minute meditation)

- Find a calm, quiet space where you can sit and observe the world around you (preferably outside or near a window looking outside)
- Pour a glass of your favorite tea, coffee, or cocktail to enjoy
- Eliminate all distractions. Draw your attention to the intricate flavors of the drink, and the pleasure of pulling something you enjoy into your body
- Take notice of the things happening around you. Find the things in the environment that bring you the most peace, and allow their presence with you to help you calm your mind. Become completely indulged in the moment.

Mindful Scheduling (10-minute meditation)
- Sit down with a pen and paper and center yourself with five deep breaths.
- Think about the days to come. Consider your priorities, remembering that every task is significant and an opportunity for increased mindfulness
- Ask yourself, "Am I giving myself adequate time to bring mindfulness and intentionality into each of these activities?"
- Take notice of any activities you feel you won't be able to be fully present for. Consider taking a thing or two off the list and saving them for a better time.
- Take notice of any feelings of stress, nervousness, or rush you feel in regards to your schedule. Breathe into those feelings.

- As you continue to write your schedule, allow yourself to feel empowered, in control, and prepared to be mindful of everything you are about to do

Mindful Driving

- Leave the house with plenty of time to be relaxed and focused. After entering the car, take a few moments to breathe and center yourself
- Once you start to drive, begin to take note of the things passing by. What do you see today that you did not see yesterday?
- Breathe in your visual surroundings, using them to center and remind yourself: "I am here. I am in this community. This is my life, and I am awake to it."

Mindful Walking (10-20-minute meditation)

- Choose an area where you can relax and bring attention to your surroundings. This can be in a park, in the city, on the beach, in your neighborhood, etc.
- Set out on your walk with no distractions
- Take notice of the things your eyes fall upon. If something specific catches your attention, allow yourself to pause and breathe it in.
- Pay attention to the sounds that surround you, giving yourself space to truly hear them

- Pay attention to the feeling of your feet on the pavement, the swing of your arms at your sides, and the rhythm of your breath
- Let your heart expand in curiosity and openness to whatever is ready to meet you in this space
- Allow yourself to become totally saturated with your surroundings, remembering that everything you see, hear, and feel is a part of you

Mindful Cooking and Eating

- As you enter the kitchen to prepare food, take a moment to center yourself in the moment with a few deep breaths
- Give every moment of the cooking process your full attention, from washing, to cutting, to cooking. Become fully immersed in the process (you can do this even with simple meals, like mindfully spreading peanut butter on bread)
- Breathe loving-kindness into the cooking process, remembering that the food you make will provide nourishment to yourself and others
- Once the food is ready, clear the eating space of distractions. Avoid multi-tasking
- Chew every bite of food 20-30 times, letting yourself be engulfed in the flavor and practicing gratitude for the nourishment
- Walk away from your meal feeling truly nourished and renewed

Mindful Waiting
- The next time you're trying to distract yourself at the doctor's office, the mechanic, or waiting for a friend or colleague to arrive, remind yourself that waiting is one of the most sacred times to engage in mindfulness
- Breathe into the moment, becoming aware of what surrounds you
- Bring awareness to your body. How are you feeling? Take note of any sensations
- Become aware of the thoughts that come once you stop numbing yourself with distractions. What things are running through your mind?
- Pay attention to the deeper thoughts you may have previously been ignoring. Ask yourself what you can learn about yourself and your life, or if there are any actions you need to take.

Mindful Creativity (at least 5 minutes)
- Set aside anywhere from five minutes to several hours of undivided time
- Engage in a creative project like art, writing, dancing, etc.
- Bring full presence to the creative project and try to eliminate all expectations. Allow the moment to carry you.
- Pay attention to how your mind and body react as the moment carries you. How do you feel?
- Examine what you create as a result of this free-flowing creativity

Mindful Play

- Dedicate time each week to doing something truly fun—something that makes you feel like a kid again (climbing a tree, swimming in the lake, drawing with chalk, baking cookies, having a game night, etc.)
- Eliminate all distractions and allow this to be a moment to step away from your everyday life and responsibilities
- Allow yourself to become lost in the childlike joy of play. Laugh loudly, let your body dance, be curious.
- Let the feeling of childlike joy saturate your body and carry this joy with you as you move back into your daily life.

Mindful Movement (10-30 minutes)

- Choose one of your favorite forms of movement (swimming, walking, dancing, going to the gym, etc.) and dedicate at least ten minutes to it
- As you begin to move, establish a deeper sense of body awareness. Pay attention to the feelings in your body as you begin to warm up and exercise
- Pay attention to the way your heart beats, your lungs heave, your face begins to sweat, and your body tingles with the sense of being alive
- Thank your body for all it does for you.

Mindful Listening/Quality Time

- Apply this meditation to any quality time you spend with another person, whether that is grabbing coffee or going for a walk with a loved one, interacting with co-workers, are conversing with the grocery store cashier
- Before interacting with others, bring attention to your levels of empathy. Set the intention to hold space for other people and the moments you share with them
- Eliminate distractions (like technology) and allow yourself to put everything else going on in your life on pause in order to be fully present
- One of the best ways to show love for people and to cultivate personal mindfulness is through mindful listening. Focus all of your attention on the other person and what they are saying. When you ask how their day is going, be present to hear the answer.
- Do not think of what your next move will be, what you will say, or where you will go. Simply be there, showing loving-kindness, holding space, and taking it all in.

Mini Meditation Toolbox: 10 Quick and Easy Meditations to Ease Stress, Depression, Addiction, Anxiety, Pain, Distraction, and Loss Using Mindfulness

Journaling the Consciousness (10-minute meditation)
- Sit down with a journal and a pen and set your timer for 10 minutes
- As thoughts, worries, or emotions arise, immediately write them down. Do not worry about structure, grammar, or content, just write.
- When the time is up, look over what you wrote
- Ask yourself which themes seem to reoccur. Where are you feeling stress in your life? What is occupying most of your mental space?
- Close your eyes and take a few moments to breathe and meditate on the thing(s) that need your attention the most
- Open your eyes. Notice how you feel lighter and in touch with your experience

Distraction Cleanse: Clearing the Space in your Mind
- *Find a quiet place and begin to breathe*
- Ask yourself: "What is distracting me from being present right now?"
- Give space to that distraction, whether it is an invasive thought, personal emotion, or someone else's emotion

- Say to yourself: "I am letting my distractions move through me as I ground myself in the present moment. Nothing is more important than right now."
- Breathe until you feel the distraction melt away into presence and mental clarity.

Re-Writing the Moment: A Short Meditation to Ease Emotional Pain of the Past

- Sit down with a journal and a pen and set your timer for 1 minute
- Take this 1 minute to write down any moment(s) of the past which have caused you a lot of pain
- After the minute is up, choose one of the painful moments, close your eyes, and begin to imagine the moment in a safe way. Be sure to keep breathing.
- When you open your eyes, take your pen and paper and re-imagine the painful moment. What do you wish had happened? How do you wish you could think about the moment now?
- After re-imagining the painful moment, remind yourself that this is a new moment. Everyone has painful memories, but you do not have to stay in spaces of the past, which are painful for you.
- Close your eyes, take a few more breaths, and say to yourself, "I release the pain of that moment of the past. This is a new moment, and I will move with it."

Re-claiming your Inner Power: A Short Meditation to Face Addiction

- Breathe into the moment, allowing yourself to think about the implications your addiction has on your life
- Without judgment, question your addiction. Ask yourself, "What has been left empty in me that I am trying to fill with this?" Listen for any emotions or past experiences of trauma, grief, or abandonment that arise. Allow them to be there.
- Say to yourself, "Now that I understand the root of my addiction, I can begin to be set free."
- With closed eyes, begin to breathe. With each breath, imagine your addiction's hold on you weakening and weakening until eventually, you have been released.
- Move forward into your life with the idea that your addiction's hold on you is loosening, day by day.

Letter to the Lost: A Short Meditation to Address Grief and Loss

- Sit down with a journal and a pen and take five deep breaths to bring you into the moment
- Allow someone you have lost to come to mind. This can be a relationship that has ended, someone who has died, etc.
- Close your eyes and breathe into the space this person has left empty within you. Allow yourself to experience any emotions that arise.
- When you open your eyes, take a few minutes to write what you wish you could have said to that person

- After you have finished your letter, close your eyes again. Tell your grief that it is okay for it to be there. With every breath, imagine yourself moving forward in your life, released from every regret you may have with someone you've lost

In with The Positive, Out with the Negative: A Short Breathing Technique
- Find a comfortable space and prepare to use the 5-5-7 breathing technique
- Breathe in for five counts and think of something positive you want to bring into this moment (kindness, peace, wisdom, etc.)
- Hold for five counts, allowing this positive thing to fill your body
- Exhale for seven counts, thinking of something negative you want to release from your body in this moment (stress, tension, selfishness, etc.)
- Begin again with a second emotion. Do this as many times as you like until you feel well-equipped with positive emotions and have released all negative ones

Space to Breathe: A Short Meditation to Gain Control over your Anxiety
- When you begin to feel anxious, step away, take a breath, and ground yourself in the moment by finding one thing you can see, one thing you can hear, and one thing you can feel. Focus deeply on each thing.

- Allow your anxiety space to exist. Remember, anxiety is the reaction your emotional brain has when it senses a threat. You can bring yourself back from catastrophe mode by using the rational brain to repeatedly remind yourself: "I am safe. I am in control. I am capable of being calm."
- Keep breathing and saying these rational-brained affirmations until you begin to feel your anxiety melt away
- Move into the next moment feeling calm, anxiety-free, and empowered

Emotion Coding: A Short Meditation to Bring you in Touch with your Emotions

- Find a quiet, comfortable place where you can easily connect with yourself
- Close your eyes and breathe deeply (you may use a breathing pattern if desired)
- Begin to travel inwards. Say to yourself, "I am ready to accept the emotions that are here."
- Wait patiently, focusing on the breath, and observing every emotion that rises to the surface.
- When an emotion arises, ask yourself a series of questions:

    1. "Is this emotion mine or someone else's?"
    2. "Does this emotion serve me or hold me back?"
    3. "What is this emotion trying to teach me?"
    4. "Should I release this emotion or put it into action?"

- When it comes to answering each question, listen to your intuition. The answers to each question are already within you. Do not question your natural answers.
- If you are being told to release an old or negative emotion, or an emotion that belongs to someone else, breathe and imagine it melting away with every exhale
- If you are being told to foster a positive emotion or a strong emotion that can create positive change in the world, sit with that, breathing, and being open to how that emotion can be useful.

The "I Love..." Gratitude Meditation (2-minute meditation)
- Find a private space, preferably one in front of a mirror
- Start a timer for 2 minutes
- For two minutes, speak out loud sentences of gratitude beginning with the words "I love…" ("I love my partner," "I love coffee," "I love my cat," "I love sunflowers," I love my mom," "I love to dance," "I love that I am healthy,").
- Say as many things as you can, one after the other. Do not think too much, simply let the things you love flow from your lips
- When the timer goes off, look in the mirror and say "And I love you," to yourself
- Feel the magic of gratitude transforming your life, your self-confidence, and your ability to be mindful

The Mindful Manifestation: A Short Meditation to Manifest what you Want in Life

- Sit down with a journal and pen
- Begin to cultivate mindfulness by bringing attention to your breath and any sensations in your body
- Ask yourself the question: "What do I want most in life?"
- As the answers start to come, open your eyes and begin to write your desires with the words "I manifest…" in front of them ("I manifest empathy." "I manifest peace of mind." "I manifest protection." "I manifest safety." "I manifest love." "I manifest awareness." "I manifest wisdom." "I manifest pure joy.")
- With each manifestation, close your eyes, and say it to yourself at least three times. Feel this manifestation become a part of your reality.

PART V

Chapter 1: Understanding Panic Attacks and Panic Disorders

Imagine the fear of watching a giant wave coming roaring towards you, while you stand frozen, unable to move an inch.

It is frightening. Have you ever experienced any such fear?
Imagine having extreme breathing difficulty all of a sudden, like having an asthma attack, without suffering from asthma.

It's scary and suffocating. Have you been in any such situation ever?
Imagine being in a situation when you are quite sure that you are not going to survive that crisis; only there is no such crisis.

It is a terrible experience. Have you been through it?
These are real-life situations that a panic attack might look like. To an onlooker, a panic may look like an overreaction. Most people consider panic attacks as dodging tactics using which you can escape facing tough situations. However, they are unable to understand that during a panic attack, the victim experiences difficulty in breathing, the actual feeling of an allergic reaction is there.

For many victims, there is a feeling of the throat closing up, feels like throat tightening, and it seems like a reaction of a body as if you were about to die, nausea, heart palpitation, excessive sweating, blackouts, chest pain, and complete loss of control are some of the common symptoms panic attack victims may experience during the attacks.

Panic attacks can come out of the blue without a prior warning or even without triggers. They are scarier than they sound because the panic attack victim can feel them approaching because there's nowhere to run. The warning signal is coming from the inside, and you can't run away from yourself.

Many people start saying breathe deeply, relax, or be calm, but all these suggestions are useless because the words don't reach the effective areas. Deep breathing can help the victim relax and avoid panic attacks, but that advice and assurance must come from inside. The realization that you can avert the attack by simply diverting your mind and staying calm must be there in you. There is no doubt that a panic attack victim would have to work on developing this confidence and realization, but it is very much possible.

What Is a Panic Attack?

Excessive anxieties and fears can lead to panic attacks. During a panic attack, the victim can experience several symptoms like racing heart, heart palpitation, excessive shaking, breathing difficulties, and nausea. Things simply start slipping out of control, and the victim starts feeling very helpless and vulnerable. Every panic attack victim doesn't experience all the symptoms mentioned above. As per the Diagnostic and Statistical Manual of Mental Disorders, fourth edition, if a victim experiences any of the four symptoms from the list given below, the victim is considered to have experienced a panic attack.

The real tell-tale sign of a panic attack is that it builds up rapidly. A person could be doing fine just a few minutes ago, and all of a sudden can start exhibiting signs of fear, anxiety, pain, and discomfort. A panic attack generally reaches its peak within ten minutes of the beginning.

Important Symptoms, the Victim of a Panic Attack, Is Likely to Experience:

(A person experiencing at least four of the symptoms at the same time is classified as experiencing a panic attack.)

1. Sensations of shortness of breath or smothering
2. Palpitations, pounding heart, or accelerated rate of heart
3. Trembling or shaking
4. Feeling lightheaded, unsteady, dizzy, or faint
5. Fear of losing control or going crazy
6. Chills or hot flushes
7. Sweating
8. Feeling of choking
9. Discomfort or chest pain
10. Nausea or abdominal distress
11. Fear of dying
12. Paresthesias (tingling sensations or numbness)
13. Derealization (a sense of unreality) or depersonalization (feeling detached from oneself)

As mentioned above, panic attacks symptoms appear very fast and do not allow the victim to understand much. It can peak within a short span of just 10 minutes, and hence initially, the victims generally do not get a chance to react properly.

A panic attack can make the victim feel like he/she isn't going to survive it. To some, the acute chest pain looks like a heart attack, and to others, the breathing difficulty episodes brought by panic attacks resemble asthma attacks. Most victims end up in emergency rooms only to be told later on that they had a panic attack.

It is important to understand that panic attacks don't last very long. A panic attack can begin out of the blue without a trigger and may reach its peak within 10 minutes. However, in most cases, panic attacks get resolved within half an hour. It is rare for a panic attack to last an hour.

Although panic attacks may last only for half an hour, for the victim, this duration may seem like an eternity. The whole period is physically and emotionally very stressful and overwhelming. It is the extreme stress experienced during the panic attack that may make it feel like a very long period, and it can be emotionally churning.

It is very important to note that there is no specific cause of panic attacks. Panic attacks can be caused by various stressors, and the genetic buildup of a person can make a person prone to panic attacks. However, people with mood disorders and long-standing anxiety issues are naturally soft-targets of panic attacks. Severe stress, major transitions in life, a feeling of acute vulnerability, and several medical conditions can also make a person prone to panic attacks.

What Is Panic Disorder and Should You Be Worried About It?

Panic disorder is having an extended fear of panic attacks all the time, even when you haven't had a panic attack in a month or more.

It is very much possible for a person to just have one or two episodes of panic attacks and then never have them ever. You were passing through a bad patch in life that made you insecure and vulnerable and caused a panic attack. When then phase passes away, you might not experience a panic attack ever again. Unfortunately, some people experience repeated panic attacks, and they undergo substantial behavioral changes making anxiety a part of their lives. They are always anxious about the next attack to come. Such people can be termed as suffering from **Panic Disorder**.

Symptoms That a Person Might be Developing Panic Disorder are:

- Constant worry about panic attacks
- Frequent episodes of panic attacks out of the blue
- Clear avoidance of things and situations that might have led to a panic attack

Panic disorders are the quiet periods between panic attacks, and they can be more harmful than panic attacks as they can severely affect the life and functioning of the victim. They can be as threatening as the silence before a storm, and that's what keeps the victims on edge.

Emotionally, panic disorder can take a toll on the mental health of the victim as it keeps the mind full of fearful thoughts and anxieties. Finding a diversion can get difficult in such a condition. The victims are unable to push the fear of an attack from their mind, and they are always in fear of an impending attack.

Chapter 2: Anxiety and Panic Attacks Aren't the Same

There are many common symptoms in anxiety and panic attacks, and that makes people draw a misleading conclusion that having anxiety disorders and panic attacks or panic disorders is all the same.

Very Important

You must make it very clear in your mind that having a panic attack is an easily treatable condition. If you've just had a few episodes of panic attacks, you can just go to a doctor and get treatment for that. A simple medication routine of a fortnight can help you get over panic attacks. However, treatment of anxiety disorders is a very lengthy process that may take years while using both medication and therapy.

Therefore, if you or someone you know just had a panic attack, there is no reason to worry as it is a treatable condition.

Differentiating between both the conditions can be a bit tricky and may need professional help.

However, here are some broad points that can help you understand the difference:

- Anxieties are generally very specific. There are triggers for anxiety. You know the things that can make you feel anxious. There would be specific stressors and triggers that can trigger anxiety in you. On the other hand, panic attacks usually come without a trigger.

- A big difference between anxiety and panic is the way you feel them. Panic attacks are sudden and intense. A panic attack can start all of a sudden without a trigger and would reach its peak in a short span of 10 minutes. Although they are fast and intense and the entire duration of a panic attack may seem like an eternity, usually they don't last longer than half an hour and would rarely extend for an hour. Whereas anxiety can keep building for months.

- Initially, the anxiety would be less, and it can keep intensifying over a long period. As time passes, your anxiety would keep getting stronger, and it simply doesn't pass away like a panic attack.

- Anxieties are usually followed by a long period of worries. It keeps the mind occupied and leads to overthinking and development of deep fear. Panic attacks end fast, and you will feel all the pressure and fear melting away. You'd feel the intense weight being lifted from your head.

Generalized anxiety in this way is much more dangerous and complex than sporadic episodes of panic attacks. It can last for anywhere between a few minutes to your whole lifetime.

However, every fear and anxiety is not bad. Generally, we feel anxious about things we are not comfortable with. When we are anxious, there can be a rapid pounding of heart, increased pulse, sweating, and tension. You get a general feeling of your inability to cope with a certain situation, and hence defensive mechanism gets activated. Most of the time, people choose to avoid things and situations that may cause anxieties. But, that's not possible in the case of panic attacks as they can come without any such trigger or stressor.

Anxiety disorders should never be ignored as they form the basis of several complicated conditions like social anxiety disorder (SAD), obsessive-compulsive disorder (OCD), posttraumatic stress disorder (PTSD), generalized anxiety disorder (GAD), etc.

Chapter 3: Biological and Psychological Causes of Panic Attacks

Biological Causes of Panic Attacks

There is a lot about the brain and its functioning that modern medical science is yet to discover. We know a lot of things, and we are still in the process of finding out a lot more things. The exact physiological causes of panic attacks are also among the few things medical science is trying to find more about.

The science known until now strongly suggests that panic attacks are caused by the faulty alarm system in our brain.

There is an area in the brain known as Locus Ceruleus. This region has a high concentration of adrenaline-like neurons. The impulse conductors of the nerve cells connect this part to:

- The cerebral cortex (the part of the brain determining intelligence, personality, motor function, senses, etc.)
- The limbic system (responsible for our emotions and higher mental function)
- Thalamus (part of the brain managing pain and emotions)
- Hypothalamus (controls the nervous system and hormone signals)

Effectively, any activity in this part of the brain is going to affect your overall functionality.

This locus ceruleus region and the adrenaline-like neurons can stimulate your body to release hormones that can activate a severe 'fight or flight response.' The body needs this hormone when it is in any kind of danger.

When in danger, the body pumps in adrenaline or epinephrine can make you feel very frightened. In a real-life dangerous situation, that the glucose supply to the cells would be stopped, and all the glucose in the bloodstream would be made available to generate maximum thrust for any action. This simply means that when you are in some grave danger, the power and thrust available to get out of that danger goes up considerably.

This of a scenario where you come face to face with a wild animal. The animal is a quadruped, and hence it has a higher speed than you. In a normal situation, there is no chance for you to outrun that animal. However, due to a very high adrenaline rush in your blood and the resulting fight or flight response, you'll be able to run much faster than your normal capacity to manage survival. This rush is shortlived. It is not possible to manage that speed in normal circumstances, but our body makes a desperate attempt to survive.

This system is there to amplify the chances of survival in dangerous circumstances. Our ancestors had to survive in the wild with no claws, horns, or brute force, whereas the animals were faster, more powerful, and had the accessories like claws, big teeth, and horns. That could make survival difficult, and hence this system was very helpful.

The alarm bells in the locus ceruleus region activate the adrenaline-like neurons, which cause a noradrenergic overload. This is a helpful process in threatening situations. However, in the case of a panic attack, this process gets activated without any stressor or danger trigger. Not only this alarm system gets activated falsely, but it is also very severe in response sending the victim in a state of panic.

Available knowledge and data suggest that this alarm system in our brains is prone to malfunction. Like any alarm system, one or two episodes can occur and then never happen again. This is a reason some people may experience panic attacks once or twice in their lives, never to experience them ever again. Even if you get a panic attack, there is nothing to worry about as just the alarm system has gone off, and otherwise, there is no threat to the body in general. This is a reason panic attacks require no hospitalization or medical care. As there is little understanding of the system, all the causes of the malfunction are not clear, but data shows that hereditary predisposition can make a person prone to such attacks.

There is a high probability that you might have heard the term serotonin. It is commonly used in connection with the things that bring a calming effect to the mind. Instantly after your body has had passed through a severe crisis, you'd notice a feeling of complete relaxation. This feeling of complete relaxation, calm, and peace is brought upon by the effect of serotonin. It is a neuromodulator that helps in modulating anxiety. Gamma-aminobutyric Acid (GABA) is also a neuromodulator chemical. Through several studies, scientists have concluded that when there is a chemical imbalance in the brain, causing low levels of GABA and serotonin, it can lead to panic attacks.

Most theories suggest that the physiological cause of a panic attack somewhere lies in the chemical imbalance in the brain and the faulty alarm system that evokes a crisis response. However, the good thing in these studies is that they suggest this fact with clarity that although the alarm system might be faulty, there is no problem with the basic functioning of the mind and the body.

This means that panic attacks are not a danger for the body. Hence, you don't need to rush to the emergency room every time you have a panic attack or something similar to that. If you could just relax and stay calm, the surge of emotions being experienced by you would pass without an incident.

However, this is easier said than done. The kind of crisis a panic victim feels is only known to that victim. The fear is debilitating. It reduces the victim to nothing. It tears down the personality of the victim. The victims may also face social humiliation due to their sudden reactions. There is no way a panic attack victim can choose the place and time of a panic attack, and that is a reason most victims develop a fear of being in public.

Psychological Causes of Panic Attacks

Panic attacks are strong fear signals being generated in your brain, and your thinking can have a major role to play in that. The kind of temperament you have, the kind of people you socialize with, the kind of job you do, the state of your financial security, etc. are some of the things that can also have a major role in a panic attack.

If any of these things are leading to any kind of insecurity, you can be at risk of a panic attack. You must remember that any kind of major stress in life can lead to a panic attack, and hence leading a balanced life is important.

If you are a person who is sensitive to negative emotions or who cannot handle stressful events, you must work on this aspect of life along with someone who is encouraging and supporting. Fear of things that are very stressful for you can also lead to panic attacks.

Major life events like the demise of a loved one, childhood experience of physical or sexual abuse, or any other such traumatic event recently can also lead to panic attacks.

Abuse of drugs and alcohol can also lead to panic abuse.

Chapter 4: Who Is At a Greater Risk of Panic Attacks?

Anyone can have panic attacks. This is a problem that can strike anyone. Even the marines, who are fitter than the fittest, can suffer from panic attacks. Therefore, if you are fortunate enough to not have experienced any, all you can do is remain cautious. You must remember that even if a panic attack comes, it is a treatable condition.

However, if you fall under any of these categories, you should remain more cautious:

- **Women:** Unfortunately, women have twice the risk of having a panic attack as compared to men. If you are a woman with claustrophobia or any other anxiety disorder, then also your risk of having a panic attack is very high. You'll need to be extra cautious about the things that can cause severe stress.

- **People between 20-29 Age Group:** Although panic attacks can come in any age group, people in the age group of 20-29 years are more likely to experience panic attacks. However, that doesn't mean that people in the younger or older age groups are immune. It can strike at any age.

- **People with a Family History:** As we have already discussed it, if you have someone in your close family with a history of panic attacks or other mental conditions, your risk of having panic attacks can go up.

- **Stressful Life-events:** If you've been through some very stressful life events such as job loss, failure in any big competition, rejection in something crucial, marriage or divorce, or history of abuse, then also the risk of a panic attack will increase.

- **Anxious or Overthinking Attitude:** Some people have anxiety in their attitude. They are never able to feel safe. They always have a lingering fear that something might go wrong. This feeling is even more overpowering when they are sitting at some very pleasant and secure place. It is their mind at play, all the time. Such people are naturally predisposed to panic attacks.

- **Mental Health Illnesses:** If a person has been struggling with generalized anxiety disorder or depression, then the risk of panic attacks will increase.

- **History of Substance Abuse:** Any person with a history of substance abuse will be at a higher risk of panic attacks. Alcohol disorders will also increase the risk many times over.

Chapter 5: Tips to Cope With Panic Attacks When They Strike

You must accept the fact that panic attacks can come. The biggest problem with panic attack victims is that they can't come to terms with the fact that they have panic attacks.

You must realize that you've had a panic attack, and it's okay to have one. You are not the first one and for sure not the last one to have one. Therefore, the best thing to do is to be calm as it is just a phase, and it'd pass away.

Many a time, when someone has a panic attack, the people standing around ask the victim to breathe deeply or be calm and that never really works. It doesn't mean that deep breathing or staying calm are not effective techniques. The victim is simply not in a condition to hear or understand these things. The power to comprehend things said by others during a panic attack goes down. But, if you train your mind and understand the power of deep breathing and other relaxation techniques, you can effectively avoid panic attacks or minimize their severity.

We'll deal with two things in this chapter:

1. Ways to Prevent Panic Attacks
2. Ways to Cope with Panic Attacks

Ways to Prevent Panic Attacks
- **Practice Breathing Exercises:** This is probably one of the most important advice you'll ever hear in panic attack prevention. When

having a panic attack, the biggest problem faced is breathlessness. The brain starts getting devoid of oxygen. If you practice deep breathing exercises, you'll be able to prevent panic attacks to a great extent. Breathing exercises are very easy and won't take longer than a few minutes of your time daily. You can practice yoga asanas as they are especially very helpful in preventing panic attacks.

- **Light Exercises**: Exercise has a very positive impact on the brain. When you exercise, the body releases hormones called endorphins that help you in relaxing and also induce a happy mood. Regular exercise can promote a sense of positivity in you and help in preventing panic attacks. However, you must remember that this usually helps when you do light exercises. When you are doing strength training and other accelerated stuff, you must be careful when you are hyperventilating as it can trigger a panic attack. In such a circumstance, your priority must remain to catch your breath first.

- **Manage Blood Sugar Levels:** Keeping your blood sugar levels managed is also a way to prevent panic attacks.

- **Avoid Stimulants like Caffeine, Nicotine, and Alcohol:** Most people know that drug abuse can lead to panic abuse, but a large number of people find it hard to believe that excessive amounts of caffeine, nicotine, and alcohol can also trigger panic attacks. You must try to avoid these.

- **Cognitive Behavioral Therapy (CBT):** This therapy can help you identify and change negative thought patterns leading to panic attacks.

Ways to Cope With Panic Attacks

- **Accept and Recognize:** Panic attacks are short, and they are harmless. You must realize the fact that the episodes you experience don't last long. No matter how bad you might feel at that moment, panic attacks pass, and you are safe again. Therefore, there is no need to fear panic attacks or to stay in denial. If you are having a panic attack, you must recognize it. Once you learn to recognize and accept the fact that you are having a panic attack, it'd be easier to understand that they will pass safely.

- **Deep Breathing:** Breathing deeply while you are having a panic attack is always helpful. Shortness of breath or breathing difficulties are common symptoms of panic attacks, and hence deep breathing will not only help in getting over the panic attacks, but it might even prevent a full-blown panic attack even from happening.

- **Inhale Lavender:** Lavender is a stimulant that can help you feel relaxed. If you get panic attacks frequently, you can keep lavender with you and smell a bit of it when having an attack, and it can help you feel relaxed faster.

- **Medication:** Some medications can help you in coping with panic attacks. If you are having panic attacks frequently, you must consult a doctor and take medication for it.

- **Avoid External Stimuli:** Many a time, loud noise in the background, bright lights, or any other kind of stimuli can also accelerate a panic attack. If you feel a panic attack coming, try to find a peaceful place as it can help you focus inwards, and you'll be able to cope with the panic attack better.

- **Try Meditation Techniques:** Meditation is a great way to train your mind to remain peaceful and calm. It is an effective technique to make your mind avoid fearful thoughts or to divert attention from them. If you can practice meditation for a few minutes daily, you'll be able to overcome the problem of panic attacks to a great extent. There are several meditation forms and techniques that you can try. Some of the effective ones are given below:

    o **Mindfulness Meditation:** Most of our panic attacks are either fuelled by our memories of the past or the fears of the future. We are seldom scared of the present as we rarely live in the present. This meditation technique can help you train your mind to live in the present or live mindfully. It can become an effective tool to cope with panic attacks.

    o **Diversion of Mind:** During panic attacks, the mind gets focused on a negative thought. If you can focus your attention on a physical point in front of you and meditate only on that point bringing your complete awareness on it, you will be able to prevent or get over the panic attack faster as your mind will get diverted.

    o **Muscle Relaxing:** Stiffening of muscles and sensation of pain can also act as a trigger for a panic attack. Practicing progressive-muscle relaxation meditation can help you in relaxing the whole body, and it also takes away the mind from fearful thoughts.

- **Picture a Happy Place:** Guided meditation using imagery of a happy place that you can imagine will also help you in coping better from panic attacks. When your mind is thinking about a happy place, it is very relaxed and calm.

- **Use Positive Affirmation:** You can use positive affirmations during a panic attack to reassure yourself that the panic attack will pass shortly without any incident. Positive affirmations like, 'this is a phase, it'll pass,' or 'you are doing fine, there is nothing to worry' can help you in dealing with the panic attacks better.

Chapter 6: The 8-week Plan to Deal With Panic Attacks

Fighting your fears can be a life-long journey. The fears are not physical; they reside in our minds. The more we think about them, the more intense they get. This chapter would help you understand the ways to tackle the things that have been scaring you for all these years.

The plan has been divided into 8 weeks. 1 week for each plan. During that week, you'll have to work only on that specific issue. You may not be addressing the whole problem, but it'll help you in dealing with the issue in the end.

You must understand that the psychology of fear can be ingrained deep inside your mind, and hence it may take you much longer than 8 weeks too. However, no matter how long it takes, if you follow these 8 steps, you'll be able to get the fear of panic attacks due to specific stressors out of your mind.

Week 1

Identify the Triggers, Fears, and Problematic Behavior

When dealing with any kind of problem, it is very important to understand that problem clearly. The biggest problem with panic attacks lies in the fact that you do not know the things causing them. However, that doesn't mean that you are completely oblivious to your fears. Your panic attack is just a sum-total of your fears. If you can identify and address your fears correctly, you'll be able to get rid of them.

Our fears are not random. They originate from various sections of our lives. We may have a fear of things related to work, education, social interaction, or any specific part of these. Once you identify those fears or triggers, dealing with them would be considerably easy. During the first week, you need to analyze every area in your life and note down the things that may be causing stress, fear, or panic. You should be as detailed as possible in this.

Main Areas of Concern:

Work-Related: Most people feel stressed at work. Although that may not cause a panic attack in every individual, there can be some people who might feel highly stressed at their workplace. You should think of all the things at the workplace that make you feel stressed. Try to be very specific. Like if you feel a sense of panic while being called to give a presentation, you must note it down.

Social Interaction: This is another area where many people feel highly insecure. Some people have anxieties about social interaction, and it can cause a panic attack. You must evaluate if social interactions invoke such a reaction in you. Try to be very specific and focused here. Think of the things that might make you feel nervous. Like if being called to sign in a function makes you feel anxious. Most people will feel nervous in that situation, but do you feel a fight or flight response kicking in?

Health and Well-being: People can get anxious thinking about their health or the health of a family member. Think if you have any fear related to that.

Relationship: Think of your fears related to your existing or past relationships and if they are making you feel anxious.

Other Factors: Think of any other fear that might be lingering deep inside you. There can be many other kinds of fears in mind. Some people are afraid of snakes and scorpions; others are scared of allergies; some are scared of heights. Think of the issue that keeps lingering in your mind.

PinPoint the Issue: You must single out the issue. When you have the problem in view, it is always easy to deal with it. Do not try to limit your entry to any specific thing. List all your fears. Try to know everything that has the potential to make you feel anxious or bring a panic attack.

Week 2

Identify Your Negative Thought Patterns

Once you have the list of things that make you fearful, you can move ahead to deal with the thoughts that lead to such fears. The fears do not come from outside. They are an exaggeration of the thoughts we have about them. Some people may faint when asked to give a speech in front of a gathering while others feel themselves at ease doing so. The task was the same for both, but their minds were working in different ways. The fearful mind started thinking about the consequences of giving that speech like being ridiculed, laughed at, talked about behind the back, saying something unreasonable, etc. The fearless mind saw an opportunity to gain popularity and express views. The situation was the same, but different minds made different assumptions and conclusions. You need to keep in mind that the assumptions made by both could have been wrong. The fearless speakers may have got booed; it happens all the time. However, the fearful speakers would have never reached the podium of completed the speech because the presumptions were incorrect, to begin with.

Our fears are caused by our thoughts, and hence it is important to identify negative thought patterns in the mind to deal with those fears.

Negative thought patterns can be classified in the following broader terms:

Unhelpful Thoughts: These are the thoughts that lead to doubts as you start thinking anything. If you are thinking of undertaking a journey, they'll lead you to think about accidents or bad things that may happen on the journey. If you are thinking of applying for a job, these thoughts will make you think about getting rejected and make you experience that feeling. You must identify if you have unhelpful thoughts very often.

What if Thoughts: These are the thoughts that try to analyze every situation. It may seem logical to think of all the sides of the coin, but it isn't as simple as that. These thoughts will lead you to emphasize on the negative outcomes.

Critical Thoughts: These are the thoughts that make you look at the negative side of everything. You become critical of your abilities, and this can start making you feel insecure, leading to panic attacks.

Victimizing Thoughts: These are the thoughts that make you feel like a victim in every situation. The victim mentality can be very dangerous as it kills all kinds of initiative. It makes you feel exploited and vulnerable, and it can lead to panic attacks. You must identify if you have victimizing thoughts.

Know the Way You Think: To solve any problem, you must know the problem first. Your thoughts are the fuel that leads to the rocket of fear that takes you on panic trips. If you want to avoid panic attacks, it is pertinent that you identify your thought pattern. You must know the way your brain thinks, and then only you will be able to make a strategy to break that thought pattern.

Week 3 and 4

Dissociate From the Negative Thought Patterns

Once the task of identifying negative thought patterns has been completed, you need to devise strategies to change those thought patterns. This may take even longer than two weeks.

Thought patterns develop over a very long period. You may have been practicing the same thought pattern since your childhood. Most thought patterns are picked from the surrounding. This solid conditioning makes the breaking of thought patterns a tough and time-consuming task as you'd need a lot of practice.

However, the only way to do this is to practice it over and over again to make this thought pattern a habit.

Practice Labeling Your Thoughts: This is the first thing that you must do. You learn to label the thought. When you have a negative thought in your mind, learn to label it as 'just a thought.' Our mind is conditioned to consider such thoughts as facts since once it is considered a fact, it is easy to believe. You'll have to identify every negative thought and label it as just a thought, and then it'd be easier to work with it. It wouldn't ring in your brain as the gospel truth.

Make It Funny: If there is any such thought that is making you feel insecure, or which is intimidating you, try to say that out in a funny tone. This simple exercise would help you make light of it. That thought wouldn't remain very fearful or intimidating.

Push Positive Thinking to that Thought: Most negative thoughts become powerful because they never get countered by a positive thought. Try countering the negative thought in your mind with a positive idea.

Evaluate that Thought: You must grade every thought as helpful or unhelpful and discard unhelpful ideas. Once you start grading your thoughts, it'd be easier for you to distance yourself from negative thoughts. They wouldn't have command over your mind.

Find time in the future to ponder over it: If any specific thought is still lingering in your mind, find a time in the future to think it over and get it out of the way. Breaking negative thought patterns should be your focus. If there is any thought that's causing trouble in your mind, either counter it positively or get it out of the mind for the time being.

Week 5

Facing the Fears Head-on

Fear is our biggest enemy. Once you have broken the negative thought pattern, your mind will be able to think about things in a much better way. Yet, it may not be ready to shun all fears. If you are faced with situations that filled you with a sense of anxiety previously, they'll have the same impact again. The correct way to face fears is to experience and overcome them. However, this can't be done without preparation.

Facing Fears in a Safe Environment: The best way to move in this direction is to face your fears in a safe environment. If you feel that you have an intense fear of public speaking, begin by speaking only in front of a small group of your friends. When you see that you have a familiar group of faces that is even encouraging you, it'll be easier to give your first speech. Give a few speeches like than and then begin expanding the circle. Include a few people who are friends of friends and then strangers. When you move in a step-by-step manner in a safe environment conquering any fear becomes possible. The key is not to expose yourself to the fearful situation all at once but to do that gradually.

Week 6

Practice Relaxation

Completely relaxing the mind is the key to overcoming panic attacks, but this is just not a psychological process as there is biology involved too. As we have discussed, panic attacks can have some severe symptoms like shortness of breath, nausea, chest pain, etc. All these symptoms emerge because your body has a quick and severe response to a stressor. You must learn to keep the body relaxed to manage panic attacks successfully.

These relaxation techniques can help you in dealing with panic attacks is an amazing way. Not only will you feel more relaxed, but even the recovery from a panic attack would be very much easier.

Practice Relaxation Meditation: Relaxation meditation is the best when it comes to panic relief or relieving stress. It is easy and simple.

You can practice it sitting or lying down as you feel comfortable. Just close your eyes and keep your awareness focused on a point. Keep breathing deeply and just push any thought that comes to mind. Your awareness should just focus on the point you are looking at with your eyes closed. Make everything else less important than this. This simple meditation will help you achieve a state of thoughtlessness.

Deep Breathing: This is one of the most important exercises in dealing with panic attacks or any other kind of anxiety. It is very simple and highly effective. You can follow it anywhere anytime. Whenever you feel a panic attack coming, you can start focusing on your breath and begin deep breathing. You'll see that a majority of times, you'll just not have a panic attack. Deep breathing is as simple as its name. Keep taking deep breaths in and then release your breath very slowly. You should also practice it at least once a day.

Progressive Muscle Relaxation: Stiffness of muscles is another cause of panic attacks. The pain and stiffness in the body keep getting ignored and emerges as a negative impulse. An easy way to get rid of that is to follow progressive muscle relaxation techniques. In this meditation technique, you scan your whole body through your awareness and release the pressure and anxiety built up in those areas. It gives you effective control of your body and also fills you up with a realization that there is no stress or anxiety inside you.

Meditation Using Guided Imagery: This is the best way to manage panic attacks. You can have a recorded guided meditation session using positive imagery liked by you. You'll be free to choose a location or situation of your choice. You can record it yourself or get a pre-recorded one. Whenever you fear a panic attack, you can switch on that guided meditation session, and the recollection of that happy place can help you avoid the negative thoughts that may lead to a panic attack.

Week 7

Practice Mindfulness

This week, you must practice mindfulness. Most people confuse meditation and mindfulness as being interchangeable terms, but they are not. Meditation is the art of looking inside. You don't run away from thoughts, you look inside the thoughts and try to understand them objectively. Mindfulness, on the other hand, is the practice of doing things mindfully. You stop running in an automated mode and start putting your consciousness behind every action you take.

For instance, when you eat, you pay attention to all the aspects of the food. You feel the taste, the aroma, the flavors, and the texture of the food. You pay attention to the process of eating. You chew the food properly and feel it while you chew. This process not only improves your understanding of every process, but it also helps in eliminating any kind of fear present in your mind regarding them.

Some Parts of Mindfulness Practice are:

> **Meditation:** Be meditative in everything you do. Stop doing things in an automated mode. Take cognizance of every action you take.

> **Be Observant:** Observe things more carefully and closely. Don't allow things to pass in front of you like that. Be observant of the things around you.

Stop Before Reacting: Before you react to anything, stop for a moment and think about that thing, the reaction it requires, and the kind of reaction you were going to give.

Learn to Shift Awareness: Learn the art of shifting your awareness on the object of your choice. For instance, if you are having fearful things about your flight, you should be able to fix your awareness at the swiftly moving second hand of your clock or any other such thing.

Week 8

Getting the Experience

This is the week to experience and practice all that you have learned in the past two months. The process may take a bit longer than two months in your case, but there is no need to worry as this is not to scale.

Just go out in the world and face your fear head-on.

However, you must observe the things you have been able to incorporate easily and the things that still need some work.

www.ingramcontent.com/pod-product-compliance
Lightning Source LLC
Chambersburg PA
CBHW071622080526
44588CB00010B/1233